THE LAWYER BOOK

THE LAWYER BOOK

A Nuts And Bolts Guide To Client Survival

by Wesley J. Smith

Illustrated by Barry Geller

PRICE/STERN/SLOAN
Publishers, Inc., Los Angeles
1987

To
my
Terrie,
who believed before anyone else.

SECOND PRINTING — MARCH 1987

Copyright © 1986 by Wesley J. Smith
Published by Price/Stern/Sloan Publishers, Inc.
360 North La Cienega Boulevard, Los Angeles, California 90048

ISBN: 0-8431-1569-6

ACKNOWLEDGEMENTS

No book is the product of the author alone—and this one is no exception. So, beyond "thanking everyone I have ever met in my life," I wish to acknowledge a few of the people who were of special help in its creation—both in the actual preparation of the manuscript, and in the preparation of me:

- My parents, Wesley L. and Leona Smith, who did one heck of a job.

- Maggie Valentine, who helped me to develop my intellect.

- Charles E. Alpert, Douglas E. "Ted" Elias, Harold Greenberg, Jack A. Rameson III and JoAnne Robbins, fine attorneys all, who freely shared their expertise with me.

- Lisa Marsoli, Nick Clemente, Leonard Stern and everyone at Price/Stern/Sloan Publishers, and Shirley Strick.

- Woody Allen, whose art helped give me the courage to take a big risk.

- John Albert, Linda Day, Bernie Wayne and Phyllis Michell, Harvey and Dianne Simmons and Guy Stockwell. Their support has meant more to me than they shall ever know.

- And finally, every lawyer I have ever worked with—for and against—and every client I have ever had (all of whom taught me so much).

TABLE OF CONTENTS

7. WORKIN' 9 TO ~~5~~ 8

8. KEEPING TRACK

9. RIDING HERD

10. WHEN BEST LAID PLANS GO AWRY

11. GOD HELPS THOSE WHO HELP THEMSELVES

12. PRIDE GOETH BEFORE A FALL

13. SAY WHAT?

A FINAL COMMENT

SUPPLEMENT

FOREWORD

During my years as a trial lawyer, I have represented thousands of individuals with legal problems, known in the trade as "clients." Personally, I find
the term "client" mildly offensive, a generic classification
that tends to categorize people into a monolithic whole—
but, I guess, we're stuck with it. Anyway, if you are, or
expect to be, a client, or at one time *were* a client and are
still wondering what went wrong, this book is for you.

Most clients conduct their business with lawyers from
a position of subservience. The reasons for this are
several-fold. Some experience a feeling of impotence in
the face of a well educated professional, or are intimidated by their lawyer's strong personality. Others simply
fear the unknown. Most have the sinking feeling that
they no longer control their own destiny. And virtually
all worry that they will fall victim to the unethical or
negligent conduct of their own attorney. Sadly, many do!

Within these pages, we'll be focusing on a unique and
special relationship—that important interaction that exists
between attorneys and their clients, which I have labeled,
strangely enough, the "attorney-client relationship."
(How's that for original thinking?)

In a way, the attorney-client relationship is very much
like a marriage. Two individuals come together and form
a partnership to achieve a common goal—in this case,
the solving of the client's legal problem. As in a marriage, *both* partners must be actively involved in the process. To the extent that one partner is not, the partnership

limps, increasing the probability of failure. To stretch the analogy further, when arbitrating attorney–client disputes, I have noticed that these failed relationships are usually the *fault of both the lawyer and the client.* This includes those circumstances which can only be labeled as "horror stories."

Let me give you an example. One of the most interesting* cases I have ever handled, and one of the most involving, surrounded a criminal appeal. The client had been convicted, along with several co-defendants, in a rather notorious case of fraud. However, unlike his fellow defendants, he was acquitted of the crime of conspiracy, which presented some unusual issues which could be raised on appeal. Continuing to strongly maintain his innocence, the client hired an attorney to prosecute the appeal, and paid the agreed–upon fee. Thereafter, the client would call the lawyer occasionally to ask how things were going, and was satisfied when he received assurances that "these things take time," and "all is well."

Needless to say, all was not well. The attorney never filed a necessary brief, and as a result, the client's appeal was dismissed. Unfortunately, by the time he hired me, the client had an appointment with the state prison.

Now, I can hear you asking, "How was that in any way the client's fault?" Well, I'll tell you—the client went wrong because he did not take an *active interest* in his own case—a case that literally meant the difference between liberty and prison. He never once asked the lawyer whether the lawyer had *experience* in criminal appeals (he didn't), nor exactly what the appeal entailed. Worse, when his lawyer told him, "these things take time," he never asked the magic question—"How much?" In other

*When a lawyer calls a case "interesting," you know *the client has taken it in the neck.*

words, he gave complete dominion over his future to his lawyer, and simply walked away hoping for the best. As a result, he got the worst. Luckily, the story had a happy ending, but had the client followed the advice given in this book, I truly believe he could have saved himself a lot of heartache—not to mention *a great deal of money.*

I must emphasize that the "art" of being a good client involves far more than mere self-protection. It requires an ability to communicate honestly and make decisions. Lawyers frequently complain about "good cases" that have been literally destroyed because the client refused to compromise, or did not tell the lawyer the whole story—or worse, was simply caught in a lie. Hopefully, this book will prevent that from happening to you.

What I am taking a long time to say is this—clients need to learn how to play their part, i.e., how to find the right lawyer, how to work effectively with him or her, and, if necessary, when and how to give their lawyer a swift kick in the seat. I hope to teach you these skills and more.

One last point. Do not let this book sit on your shelf gathering dust, but rather use it as a working guide to assist you, whenever you are "with lawyer." Not only will it make your life easier, but it should help your lawyer do a better job—*for you.*

Wesley J. Smith
Woodland Hills, California

INTRODUCTION

This is the clearest, best-organized and wisest book I have read for people who have to use lawyers for their personal legal problems. It is practical, lightly but accurately written and frequently witty. The author, Wesley J. Smith, is an experienced California attorney who puts himself in the mindset of clients as he asks and answers the obvious questions that occur to you when seeking legal advice or representation. Then he lets you in on what attorneys know but prefer not to tell you; issues that would not even occur to you and that therefore prevent you from asserting your rights vis-a-vis your lawyer.

Why are these observations of more than peripheral importance? Let's start with a finding by an American Bar Association study: Seventy percent of Americans forego legal advice because they do not trust lawyers or cannot afford them. Other studies have added that many people fear lawyers or are in such awe of them that the same inhibition sets in. By not going to lawyers, some people lose nothing; matters somehow work out. But other people who do not obtain legal representation lose the opportunity to use the law or the legal system to defend or secure their rights. For lawyers, through their license to practice, have what amounts to a near-monoply on using the legal system on behalf of others.

Sometimes, Bar Associations go to extremes, charging non-lawyers who help people fill out forms with the unauthorized practice of law. Other times, the Bar inflates the peril of, as Smith puts it, "going it alone." Our Public Citizen Litigation Group has fought successfully against minimum fee schedules and Bar Association rules against competitive advertising in order to diminish the legal establishment's self-regulated monopoly. In 1983, the Litigation Group also published a book entitled *Representing Yourself: What You Can Do Without A Lawyer*, by Professor Kenneth Lasson.

It is with such a background of skepticism about the indispensability of lawyers and the mystique of law that I believe Smith's short, pithy, easy-to-read volume to be so useful to the many millions of Americans who need help at the threshold of the law office — a place where they should feel informed, confident and on equal terms with the lawyer within.

Before you wonder why you need to read, digest and apply the tenets of this 240-page book, I will simply tell you this: This book is so important that you should take it to the attorney whom you choose and say to him or her: "These are the rights and standards which I want to apply to our relationship. They are written by one of your legal brethren in good standing. If you object to anything herein, please let me know now. Otherwise, I'll expect THE LAWYER BOOK to define how we shall treat each other."

You'll still have to find a good lawyer before you put the book down on his or her desk; your prospective attorney's reaction to this gesture is, in and of itself, a good test for selecting your legal advocate. You see, many lawyers, even good ones in terms of technical competence, are not ready for the consumer or client assertiveness and participation that Mr. Smith believes desirable. They have become accustomed to a one-sided, command relationship toward their client, an essentially non-accountable relationship on matters that are important to the client — meeting deadlines, accurate billing, adequate notification of the client on courses of action, the vigor of the advocacy and the like. Lawyers certainly do not, by and large, give you the impression that they work for you and that you are their boss. So you have to raise their expectations of you, i.e., your right to know and to receive competent performance. If you proceed piecemeal in an effort to gain your lawyer's respect, he or she may sense that you are going to be a troublemaker, are going to demand perfection or that you are a nagger. But when you place this book as the foundation of your relationship at the outset, these fears and wonders are not as likely to arise. For at this early point, lawyers need to know that *you know!*

Nonetheless, you need to read this book carefully. It will take you about three to four hours, and what it saves you in money and aggravation may make those hours the most lucrative ones you have ever worked — if reading this breezy but serious book is to be considered "work."

First, lawyer Smith eases you into the proper mode of finding and interviewing good attorneys. (E.g., never hire a lawyer who happens to be your cousin Ralph.) Then he builds your self-confidence with a section on your "Bill of Rights" as a client. (E.g., prompt return of phone calls and *detailed* billing statements — no vague "services rendered" scams.) Just as you are feeling more in control, he introduces you to your own responsibilities. (E.g., be prepared with the full facts of your case, be punctual, comply with your lawyer's requests so that you can help him or her to help you all the better.) Next stop on Smith's journey is the chapter on pitfalls, including the hidden expenses of lawsuits and how to keep them from going into outer space (by controlling your lawyer through an eagle eye on billing abuses and a solid Retainer Agreement).

By this time in the book, you may be hungry for "context." Enough do's and don'ts, let's have some substance on what lawyers do in this adversary system

of civil and criminal lawsuits. Smith gently introduces you
to various fields of law with examples of when you should
hire a lawyer (after indicating when you can go it alone),
which teach you a little about law as well. He even includes
a glossary of 85 words commonly used by lawyers —
jargon to outsiders — and provides "loose translations into
'normal people's language'." These translations are satiric
enough to qualify Wesley J. Smith as the potential Ambrose
Bierce of the law.

Any book like this has to be usable. Smith provides
mock scenarios of conversations between clients and
lawyers both honest and tricky. He includes sample
questions to ask your lawyer about your case which are
so practical that you find yourself saying, "Yes, I need to
get that answer!" Throughout, he gives "hints" to
punctuate and remind you of the essential point of his
advice. If you find your dealings with your lawyer need
termination, he has suggestions on what to do — all the
way to suing your lawyer or reporting him or her to the
official state disciplinary body in each of the 50 states and
the District of Columbia. He even provides a form letter
to use when firing your lawyer.

Clients are buyers of legal services and lawyers are the
sellers of these services. For too long, notwithstanding the
super-abundance of lawyers in the United States (now at
the 600,000 level), this particular marketplace, where tens
of billions of dollars are exchanged yearly, has been a
seller's market. Wesley J. Smith is saying, through this
book, that it is time for a buyer's market. He is saying that
by *not* being knowledgeable and persistent, you won't
likely know when you are being disserviced or defrauded
by your lawyer. And, more positively, he is telling you,
with ever-so-light a touch, that strong, informed clients
make for more competent and honest lawyers who, in turn,
can make the legal system more productive of justice and

more responsive to "people in need" — not just to "people in greed," who are rich enough to pay. Conservative estimates report that eighty percent of lawyers represent about twenty percent of the people. With more storefront legal clinics opening and with more prepaid legal service plans being adopted, more Americans will be treading into lawyers' offices for preventative counsel or conflict resolution. THE LAWYER BOOK provides you with a tip-of-tongue and hands-on framework for choosing a practitioner wisely and getting the most out of your choice — all the way to the resolution of your matter or dispute.

One more ingredient is necessary to make your buying expertise help your lawyer to help you: your *desire* to become a proficient buyer of legal services. Desire is cultivated by an intuitive pleasure-pain principle — when you know the score, you pay less and receive more. Like a good diet, buying expertise is a process of self-improvement; stick with it and it will work for you. So give yourself a chance to make the legal profession an obedient and effective servant — sample Wesley J. Smith's recipes for success and become a first-class client!

Ralph Nader
Washington, D.C.

1

LOOKING FOR MR. OR MS. GOODBAR

FINDING THE NAMES OF *GOOD* LAWYERS

So, you think you need a lawyer. Now, I realize that for most people, hiring a lawyer is about as much fun as getting a root canal, but remember, things could always get worse—you could hire the *wrong lawyer.*

What follows should help you avoid that mistake . . .

THE WRONG APPROACH

The following reasons should *not* be the basis of your decision to hire a lawyer:

- ## Because the lawyer ran an ad in the current issue of the *Penny Saver*

Lawyer advertising is a relatively new phenomenon, and not one that I am especially thrilled about. But since it's here to stay, a few words to the wise are in order. An advertisement by a lawyer can only tell you two things: that the lawyer could afford to pay for the ad, and the area of law in which the lawyer practices. That's it. What it doesn't tell you is whether the lawyer is a good one. And thus, while advertisements can be a source of names, an ad should not be the sole reason you make your selection.

- ## Because the lawyer happens to be your cousin Ralph

I know many of you will disagree, but *never, never, never* hire a lawyer who is a good friend or a close relative. The reasons are simple; to be effective, your lawyer must be able to stand back and view your situation objectively, and if he or she has an emotional attachment to you, his or her ability to do so may be severely compromised. In addition, you have to be able to be completely candid with your lawyer without worrying about what he or she thinks about you as a person. Having a close friend or relative representing you may inhibit your ability to speak freely. Moreover, the fact that your cousin Ralph is a lawyer doesn't mean he has the expertise to handle your particular problem. Finally, it's just too risky. Close relationships are important, and I've seen too many ruined by making a personal relationship a professional one. No, you're far better off using your cousin Ralph as a source of names, rather than hiring him. There's just too much at stake.

• Because the lawyer is famous

The fact that a lawyer is famous may have more to do with self-promotion than legal ability. Let me give you an example of what I mean. Several years ago there was a famous lawsuit involving a big name celebrity. *One* of the lawyers in the case (the famous one), constantly appeared on television to talk about the case, and gave statements to the press on a daily basis during the trial. The other lawyer refused to talk about the case at all, and instructed his client to follow his example. Well, *that* lawyer won the case—and nobody even knows his name.

Now, I'm not saying that famous lawyers aren't good; most of them are. But, their fame brings no guarantee—except, perhaps, that they will be more expensive.

- **Because a lawyer shares your religious affiliation, or is a member of the Kiwanis Club**

People want a lawyer they can trust, so it is not surprising that many clients select their lawyer just because they go to the same church or belong to the same fraternal order or service club. This can be a terrible mistake. The fact that you and the lawyer share a common interest has nothing whatsoever to do with the lawyer's ability to handle your case. Thus, while a lawyer who shares a common interest may be worth investigating, the common interest *alone should not* be the basis for your decision.

- **Because the lawyer wrote a book telling you how to find a lawyer**

But, this is stating the obvious.

A MORE ORGANIZED APPROACH

STEP 1: IDENTIFY THE PROBLEM

You don't just want a lawyer, you want a lawyer who practices in your field of legal need. For example, if you've been arrested for drunk driving, you obviously don't need a patent lawyer, so you can scratch patent lawyers off your list.

The following is a very general breakdown of the different types of law attorneys practice. Of course, a lawyer may practice in more than one of these fields, but I think it's safe to say that no lawyer practices in *all* of them.

Civil trial law

Civil trial lawyers conduct trials in cases ranging from breach of contract and will contests to real property disputes. Or, to put it another way, a civil trial lawyer is the one you call when you "want to sue the bastards," or "have been sued by the bastards."

Criminal law

If you have been accused of a crime, whether it is drunk driving or murder, or are even a "non-arrested suspect," you need a criminal lawyer. Interestingly, many of the best criminal defense lawyers are former police officers or district attorneys.

Domestic relations law

Technically, domestic relations lawyers are civil trial lawyers, but the field is growing so complex that they deserve a category all their own. Domestic relations lawyers handle divorces, dissolutions, adoptions—and "palimony" cases, in states that recognize such suits.

Business law

If you plan to buy, operate or sell a business, form a corporation, enter a joint venture, or go into partnership, you would hire a business lawyer.

Estate planning and probate law

These are lawyers who draft wills and trusts and who otherwise try to protect your estate from estate taxes upon your demise (a fancy "lawyer word" for death). Probate lawyers also frequently handle guardianships and conservatorships (as do some civil trial lawyers).

Civil law

As opposed to civil *trial* lawyers (although a civil lawyer can also be a trial lawyer and vice versa), a civil lawyer, for our purposes, concentrates on drafting contracts, interpreting legal documents and handling real estate transactions (among other things).

Administrative law

Administrative lawyers practice before government regulatory agencies, such as zoning commissions and state contractor licensing boards.

Entertainment law

These lawyers represent individuals and business entities in the entertainment industry—which includes films, television, music and publishing. You can usually tell the entertainment lawyers from "regular" lawyers—they're the ones who don't wear ties.

Workers' compensation law

These lawyers represent workers who have been injured in job-related accidents.

Tax law

Tax lawyers advise on tax implications of personal as well as business matters, and represent clients in disputes with tax authorities.

Personal injury law

Technically, "P.I." or "accident" lawyers are civil trial lawyers. But, as with domestic relations, the law of personal injury is a world by itself. This is especially true in the field of medical malpractice, because many states are making it harder to recover damages against doctors, due to pressure from insurance companies and medical associations.

Immigration law

Immigration lawyers assist aliens in obtaining permanent resident status, and deal in matters of obtaining citizenship or resisting deportation.

Patent, copyright and trademark law

I have grouped these specialized areas of the law together for simplicity's sake. All are very technical and require a lawyer with precise knowledge of the rules and regulations pertaining to each.

> **HINT:** *Due to the increasing complexity of our legal system, the day of the general practitioner is coming to an end, as it is in medicine. As a result, many State Bar Associations have begun to institute fields of specialization*—and to become a "specialist" in a given field, the lawyer is required to take special classes and pass a rigorous examination. Some lawyers advertise that they emphasize or specialize in certain fields. This is not the same as passing a State Bar test and becoming certified. If in doubt, ask.*

*For specialization information regarding your state, see supplement at the end of this book.

STEP 2: MAKE A LIST OF NAMES OF LAWYERS TO INVESTIGATE

Finding the names of lawyers is the next step—not too difficult a task, considering the number of lawyers who practice in the United States. But you want *more* than mere names—you want *recommendations*. Several sources you may want to use are:

A former lawyer

If you have had a lawyer in the past and liked the service you received, and if that attorney has experience with your current type of problem, you may wish to interview him or her for the job. If not, ask for a recommendation.

Other lawyers

Lawyers are always an excellent source of names because they usually know the reputation of their colleagues, so if you know a lawyer whom you won't be retaining (for example, your cousin Ralph), ask for a referral. In such cases, have your lawyer (friend) call and let the referred lawyer know he or she has been recommended. You just might receive a little extra attention if you do.

Relatives, friends and co-workers

People whom you are close to who have had a *problem similar* to yours can also be an excellent source. And, just as important, they can tell you which lawyers to avoid. I find such "word of mouth" recommendations to be particularly reliable.

Local Bar Associations

Most cities or counties have local Bar Associations that operate lawyer referral services at little or no cost.

Though they lack the personal touch, these services can be helpful in referring you to the kinds of lawyers you need, and if you wish, specifically to those in your community.

HINT: *Lawyers who wish to have clients referred to them by Bar Association referral services do not have to take any special test or otherwise prove the extent of their expertise in any given area. So, don't make the mistake of believing that the referral from a Bar Association is a guarantee of quality—because it isn't.*

Pre-paid legal insurance plans

For a fee, pre-paid insurance plans offer legal services at reduced rates, but because they are a relatively new phenomenon, their track record hasn't been established yet. The problem I find with most of these organizations is that you have to choose a lawyer from a pre-selected panel. If this is the case, be sure to interview a number of panel lawyers before making your final selection.

HINT: *As with Bar Association referrals, a referral by a pre-paid legal insurance plan is no guarantee of expertise—although there is usually some sort of screening process performed by the plan administration before attorneys can become a member of the panel. On the positive side, if you have a problem with a lawyer you were referred to by a pre-paid plan, you have a place where you can go to complain, and hopefully get fast results.*

Legal directories

There are several publications that list lawyers in your area. Some of these also list the fields in which they practice. Consult your local librarian for assistance.

Insurance companies

If you have been sued, and you have liability insurance, contact your insurance agent and make a claim. If you qualify, they will provide you with an attorney, and you pay only the deductible. However, just because your insurance company is paying the bill, it doesn't mean you have no say in the matter. So, if you are unhappy with its selection, *speak up!*

STEP 3: RESEARCH THE LAWYERS ON YOUR LIST

After you have a list of five or so names (make sure each lawyer practices in the area of your need), make appointments with at least three of the lawyers.

HINT: *When making the appointment, make it clear that you are going to be talking to several lawyers before selecting the one you want. Also find out the office policy on charging for initial office consultations; many lawyers give them free or at nominal cost.*

Before your appointments, you should also go to the law library at your local courthouse, or a nearby law school, and ask the librarian to give you the publication lawyers use when looking for a lawyer themselves—*The Martindale-Hubbel Law Directory.* Then ask the librarian to help you find each of the lawyers whom you will be meeting with, who should be listed within the publication. *Martindale-Hubbel* is especially helpful because it lists a lot of information about lawyers, such as:

- year of birth
- name of college and date of graduation
- name of law school and date of graduation
- year admitted to practice in your state

More important, the publication *rates* lawyers on legal expertise and ethical standards. The ratings range from "C.V." (high legal ability) to "A.V." (very high legal ability). The "V" means "very high ethics." The ratings are based upon anonymous questionnaires sent by *Martindale-Hubbel* to lawyers and judges, so they tend to be pretty reliable.

HINT: *If a lawyer is not rated by Martindale-Hubbel, it doesn't necessarily mean that he or she is not a good lawyer—in fact, the publication itself states that no unfavorable inference can be drawn. But if a lawyer you may be interested in is rated, then you will know the esteem he or she is held in by the local legal community.*

HINT: *In a separate portion of Martindale-Hubbel, lawyers "advertise"—not in the sense of some of the ads seen on television, but by giving helpful information, such as:*
- *biographical data*
- *area of emphasis*
- *specialty, if any*
- *honors, if any*

Now that you have done your research, you are ready to meet your prospective lawyers face to face.

2

THE AUDITION
INTERVIEWING PROSPECTIVE LAWYERS

T he fateful day arrives, when with dry throat and sweaty palms, you appear in a lawyer's office for what is known in legal circles as the "initial office conference." For many, this is an incredibly intimidating experience, but it doesn't have to be, and it *won't* be, if you conduct the interview correctly.

The first thing to remember is that behind the efficient secretary, behind the word processors and the eager law clerk buried under mounds of books, behind the plush office with its oak desk and high-back chair, and yes, even behind the pinstriped suit, is a human being who sincerely wants to be of service to you.

Second, remember it is the *lawyer* who is being interviewed, not you! His or her livelihood *depends* on attracting clients, and you should approach the conference as if you were hiring an employee—and in reality, isn't that exactly what you are doing?

PREPARATION FOR THE INITIAL OFFICE CONFERENCE

Alright, you have selected one of the lawyers from your list of qualified candidates, and you have made an appointment. You must now be sure you are prepared to tell your story to the lawyer in a clear and concise manner. Here are some tips that will help you.

Write down the facts of your case ahead of time

This is vital! The facts you give your lawyer at the initial office conference will be the *basis of his or her legal advice*. So, you must be as accurate and complete as you can.

> **HINT:** *Try to keep your feelings out of the written summary— they usually just get in the way.*

Gather together all relevant evidence in your possession

By evidence, I mean "objective" things that pertain to your case, such as documents (medical bills, letters, receipts, etc.) or objects (such as a pair of shoes in a "slip and fall" case). If you have documents, do yourself and your lawyer a favor—arrange them in chronological order or index them. Not only will this make his or her job easier, but it will save time—which *saves you money.*

Whatever it is, whether you think it helps or it hurts, bring it in to the lawyer. Think twice and even three times if necessary about such items, because their existence can often be the difference between winning and losing your case.

Make a list of all evidence not in your possession

Since all of the evidence may not be in your possession, you will need to list items your lawyer will have to obtain through legal processes. Try to be as organized and complete as you can.

Write down the names of all witnesses

Witnesses are vital to any lawsuit, and the sooner your lawyer interviews them the better. Thus, be sure to write down the name, address and phone number (both work and home) of all known witnesses, to give to your lawyer. You should also write down a brief statement of what each person will be able to testify to.

THE INITIAL CONFERENCE

After you have met the lawyer, and the initial pleasantries have been exchanged, the first order of business usually consists of you telling your story. Since you will have done your preparation, this should be no problem. You can either read from your notes, or, if you are really ambitious, you can mail your story in letter form to the lawyer ahead of time.

Throughout your recitation, your lawyer may interrupt with questions. Answer them to the best of your ability. When you have finished, your lawyer will give you his or her legal opinion. *Write down what you are told*, to compare with what other lawyers you interview will tell you (see sample at end of chapter). Or, even if you don't interview other lawyers, use it to put in your Duplicate File Notebook (for details see Chapter Eight).

This is about the time most lawyers get around to talking about money. The lawyer will tell you how much money he or she requires for an initial retainer (payment), if any, and how much he or she charges per hour (if appropriate). The lawyer may ask for a payment to his or her "client trust fund" to cover payment of costs. Again, *write this information down*.

By now you should have a gut feeling about whether or not you are interested in having this particular lawyer represent you. If you are *not interested*, for whatever reason, thank the lawyer for his or her time, pay whatever fee may be required (frequently lawyers give inexpensive or free initial consultations) and tell the lawyer you want to think it over.

If you feel the lawyer is a person whom you *are interested* in retaining, ask some of the following questions (and any of your own) so that you can be sure. Again, always *write down the answers.* (I know I'm a nag, but I think it's important).

Sample questions about the case

Ask for an explanation of anything or any term you didn't understand.
For example, you might ask, "You said I am probably entitled to a 'Restraining Order'. What exactly does that mean?" Remember, the more you understand, the better you are able to make intelligent decisions.

"What specific action do you recommend?"
Lawyers frequently talk in generalities about "bringing suit" or "applying pressure." Find out exactly what your lawyer means and intends to do.

"How long do you think it will take to get started?"
A very busy lawyer might take three weeks to accomplish what another lawyer can do in two days. If time is important to you, this question is vital.

"How long do you anticipate the entire process will take?"
In some states, lawsuits can take as long as five years to reach trial! You need to know the answer to this question, because you may decide it is not worth the time to go forward. In any event, you will want to prepare yourself for the time that will be involved.

"What will be happening step by step?"
Whether you are involved in a lawsuit, a purchase of property, or a drafting of a will, there is a logical step-by-step process that takes place. Find out what these steps are, and when they will occur, so that you can be prepared.

"What problems do you anticipate?"
Every legal action carries with it the possibility of problems. Find out what they may be ahead of time so you can be prepared.

"What do you believe the outcome will be?"
Even at this early stage, your lawyer will have a general idea about your chances (which, of course, are subject to change as the case develops). If he or she feels pessimistic, find out

why. You may save yourself a lot of trouble and money by electing not to proceed.

> **HINT:** *If your lawyer makes a guarantee of success—BEWARE! "Sure things" are even more rare in law than they are in real life.*

Questions about the lawyer

I firmly believe you also need to know about the prospective lawyer's professional life in order to make a well informed decision.

"How long have you been in practice?"

After my swearing in ceremony, I said to my father, "Well, Dad, I'm a lawyer!" His response surprised me. He said, "No, Son, you're not. Law school gave you the tools. You won't really be a lawyer until you learn how to use them." Dad was right. That isn't to say you should not hire a rookie lawyer—frequently his or her enthusiasm more than makes up for inexperience. But, I would think twice if my problem was complex or involved being charged with a serious crime.

"What is your experience in cases such as mine?"

A lawyer experienced in one area may be incompetent in another. Or, to put it another way, the lawyer who did a dynamite job for you when you were arrested for drunk driving, may be a dud in the divorce resulting from that arrest—so, be careful.

"How many other cases are you handling?"

Some lawyers may think this is none of your business, but I disagree. An excellent lawyer may be able to represent 100 to 125 clients without much of a problem*, but will usually begin to sink beneath the waves if he or she handles more than 150 cases without assistance. I simply believe you have a right to know whether the lawyer will have time to give you 100%.

"Will you be the only lawyer working on my case?"

Many experienced lawyers, especially in larger firms, may delegate some of the work to less experienced associates or to law clerks. There is nothing wrong with this practice, so long as you are charged a lower rate for services performed by less experienced personnel, you approve of the practice and are informed of it ahead of time, and, the lawyer you hired originally (and have a personal relationship with) bears ultimate responsibility for your case.

---

*I am talking about a trial lawyer here. Workers' compensation, probate or lawyers with other types of practices may be able to handle far more, or far less.

"Do you enjoy practicing law?"
The practice of law is a very stressful way to earn a living, and consequently many lawyers suffer "burn out." If your lawyer gives you the impression that he or she wishes he or she could be doing something else, chances are your case will not be handled with zeal—which can be the difference between victory and defeat.

"Do you continue to take courses to update your legal skills?"
The law is continually changing, and if your lawyer does not take continuing education courses from a local university or Bar organization, he or she may be behind the times.

MAKING THE CHOICE

After you have interviewed two or three prospective lawyers, you should be in a position to make an intelligent decision. While there are no magic formulas, try comparing the following qualities of the respective candidates:

Trustworthiness—Which of the lawyers you have interviewed inspired the most trust? If you don't feel you can be totally candid with a lawyer, or you don't feel completely safe with him or her, scratch that lawyer off your list.

Simpatico—Which candidate do you like as a person the most? Of course it is not necessary that you like your lawyer, but it sure helps.

Enthusiasm—Do you believe the lawyer will *enjoy* representing you? Is he or she "chomping at the bit, raring to go?" Lawyers who do not enjoy what they do usually have a harder time getting the job done.

Judiciousness—At the same time, you want the lawyer you choose to be able to stand back from the problem and look at it from all sides. If a lawyer does not have the ability to look at your problem objectively, you should look for representation elsewhere.

Assertiveness—Do you believe that your lawyer is someone who will fight for you if necessary? If not, go elsewhere.

Experience—Is the lawyer's background such that you feel confident that your case will be handled correctly? Obviously you shouldn't hire a lawyer who you don't think is up to doing the job.

Economy—What do each of the candidates charge? Balance this factor against others to find the best lawyer for you.

Ability—Which of the lawyers most inspires confidence that he or she knows what he or she is doing? Remember, regardless of desirable personality traits, an incompetent lawyer will always do you more harm than good. So, look beyond personality in making your ultimate decision.

This may seem like a lot of work, but think of what is at stake! So, do your homework, take notes and compare your candidates. You'll be surprised how easy the decision will be!

You cannot be expected to write down everything the lawyers you interview will want to know, but the following Summary of Facts Checklist and Sample Fact Summary should get you off to a good start. Do your best to be complete in the information; it will help each lawyer get a quick grasp of the case and will help you organize your thoughts, and ultimately save you money.

SUMMARY OF FACTS CHECKLIST

When you are writing down the facts of your case, be sure to include the following information.

1. **WHAT** HAPPENED
2. **WHEN** IT HAPPENED
   A. Date
   B. Time of Day
3. **WHERE** IT HAPPENED
      Locations, addresses, etc.
4. **WHO ELSE** WAS INVOLVED? WHAT THEIR STORY IS
5. **WHO** KNOWS ABOUT THE MATTER
   A. Names, addresses and phone numbers (both work and home)
   B. What each person knows.
   C. How each person knows.
      1. Where they were (specifically) at the time.
      2. Why they were there at the time.
   D. The *relationship*, if any, of the person to the principals, i.e., "my nephew," "my neighbor's son," "an independent witness to the accident," etc.
   E. What that person *said*, if anything, i.e., "I saw the whole thing. The other guy ran a red light." Or, "Leave me out of it, I don't want to get involved," etc.
6. LIST OF EVIDENCE
7. MISCELLANEOUS

SAMPLE FACT SUMMARY

Here is an example of what I mean by a good, factual summary.

1. What happened

I was driving east on Ventura Blvd. and stopped for a red light at Balboa Blvd. I suddenly heard a screeching of tires and felt a powerful impact which really shook me up.

I got out of the car and exchanged information with the driver of the other car. He was very angry and accused me of being stopped at a green light. Two women came up to me and told me they "saw the whole thing." They gave me their names and phone numbers.

I sat on the curb because my back and shoulders hurt. I felt sick to my stomach. A policeman arrived and took my statement. Finally a tow truck came and towed my car to the Ace Body Shop. I called my insurance man who filled out a claim and took pictures.

I went home and went to bed. The next day I could hardly move. My wife took me to my doctor who put me in the hospital for observation. I was given pain medication and physical therapy. Two days later I went home. I am still under treatment. I have frequent headaches, shoulder pain and my fingers tingle. I can't sit or stand for prolonged periods. I have not been able to work for three weeks and may be fired.

2. When it happened

The accident occurred on May 3, 19__, sometime after lunch. I was in the hospital from May 4 to May 6, 19__. I have not worked since May 2, 19__.

3. Where it happened

The accident occurred at the corner of Ventura Blvd. and Balboa Blvd. I went to Holy Cross Hospital, located in Granada Hills. My car was repaired at Ace Body Shop.

4. Who else was involved

The driver of the car that hit me is:
I.M. Reckless
2222 Speedster Lane
Los Angeles, CA
Phone # 999-6666
License # Y 55533

The owner of the car that hit me is:
        U.R. Disturbed
        4444 Crazy St.
        Los Angeles, CA
        Phone # 999-5555

What their story is

Reckless said I stopped for a green light. Disturbed said she never should have loaned her car to Reckless.

5. Who knows about the matter

Two witnesses:
        CLARA DO GOOD
        8686 Courage Drive
        Topanga, CA
        Phone # 444-9999
        (Said she saw the "whole thing.")

        SARA SAINT
        888 Prophet Point—Apt #7
        Topanga, CA
        Phone # 888-8888
        (Said she'd help me.)

Policeman from Van Nuys, Ca.
        Name and division unknown.
        (Took my statement and statement of driver and of witnesses.)

My doctor:
        DR. GOODFELLOW
        2222 Miracle Mile
        Los Angeles, CA
        Phone # 777-7777
        (Saw my condition after accident.)

My insurance agent:
    JOHN ALLSTATE
    4444 Hitnrun Lane
    Los Angeles, CA
    Phone # 888-0000
    (Took pictures of my car. Took my statement.)

My physical therapist:
    PETE ACUPUNCTURE
    9000 Ouch Drive
    Woodland Hills, CA
    Phone # 666-6666
    (Knows what pain I'm in.)

My wife:
    DOLLY VICTIM
    My address
    (Sees the pain I'm in.)

My employer:
    BOB BIGSHOT
    8888 Hardhead Road
    Los Angeles, CA
    Phone # 555-4444
    (Angry I'm missing work.)

6. List of evidence

A. *Pictures of my car (In insurance agent's possession)*
B. *Medical records*
C. *Doctor bills*
D. *Employment records*
E. *Police Report (with Police Department)*

7. Miscellaneous

I received a call from Reckless's insurance agent offering me $5,000 in damages. The agent's name and address are, etc.

SAMPLE: NOTES ON WHAT MY LAWYER TOLD ME

Whenever you discuss your case with your lawyer, take notes. Always include:

- **the date**
- **where** the conversation took place
- **what** your lawyer told you
- **list of your comments**

Example #1

May 16, 19___. I met with Mouthpiece A. Shyster in his office.

- *He's been in practice 10 years.*
- *Mostly handles accident cases.*
- *He recommends we try to settle the case before we sue.*
- *Says it will take 3 years to complete if we sue.*
- *Believes my case is worth $15,000 if I heal.*
- *Would try to settle right away for $15,000.*
- *Charges a flat fee of 40% of the recovery.*
- *Would file Complaint and interview witnesses within six months, if no progress toward settlement.*
- *Has 160 cases (got angry I asked).*
- *Said he loved the law.*
- *Said that the case looks like a sure thing.*
- *Said he'd do most of the work himself.*

MOUTHPIECE A. SHYSTER

Comments

I was kept waiting one hour.
He took phone calls while we talked.
He told me he was going through a divorce.
He tried to pressure me into hiring him.

Example #2

May 17, 19___. I met with Whata Gal in her office.

- *She has been in practice 5 years.*
- *She handles personal injury cases & divorce cases.*
- *She has 75 Clients.*
- *She will charge 33% before trial & 40% after trial.*
- *She believes the case is good, but a lot will depend on what the witnesses & the police report say.*
- *Can't say what the case is worth. It all depends on how I heal and what happens with my job.*

- *Does not recommend an immediate settlement because injuries like mine take time to resolve.*
- *Would file Complaint within 2 days.*
- *Interview witnesses within a week.*
- *Take depositions (testimony under oath) within 2 months.*
- *Believes the case will take 1-3 years to complete.*
- *Wants to know my past medical history.*

Comments
I liked her. She seemed to like me.
Her staff was very friendly.
She said she had a law clerk who helped her, but she said she would do most of the work.

As you can see, by comparing the notes, there is a big difference between those two lawyers. Putting your notes on paper will help you make an intelligent decision.

3

THE CLIENT'S BILL OF RIGHTS
CONDUCT YOU DESERVE FROM YOUR LAWYER

THE 3-PIECE SUITS ARE COMING!

I had a terrible nightmare the other night. I dreamed I was at the Boston Tea Party, but instead of revolutionaries throwing English tea into Boston Harbor, enraged clients were throwing in legal briefs. And then Paul Revere rode up and instead of warning about Red Coats, he yelled "The Three Piece Suits are coming, The Three

Piece Suits are coming!" Well, I woke up in a cold sweat—I mean, I didn't know which side I was supposed to be on . . .

Anyway, that got me thinking about the antagonism that exists between clients and lawyers—and the ways in which lawyers must conduct themselves to put an end to it. Thus, with apologies to the founding fathers, I hereby establish the *Client's Bill of Rights.*

RIGHT #1

Clients have the right to prompt return of phone calls

This is a matter of simple courtesy and respect. Unfortunately, most lawyers, myself included, get poor marks in this area. Now it is true that lawyers simply cannot always return your phone call on the same day it is made, but a staff member can, even if it is just to tell you that your lawyer is unavailable and to establish a mutually convenient time to communicate.

Here is a list of messages which tend to work well:

- "May I leave a message, then?"
- "It's quite important that I speak with him (her). Can you tell me when he (she) will be available?"
- "If he (she) is unable to return my call, will you or another staff member please call me so that I can leave a message?"
- "Will he (she) be phoning in for messages? Please tell him (her) it is urgent that we speak. I can be found at (phone #) until noon and at (phone #) until four o'clock. He (she) can also call me at home tonight (phone #) whenever he (she) is available.
- "There is no rush. Have him (her) call me when it is convenient."

- "He (she) hasn't returned my last three phone calls. Please tell him (her) I would appreciate the courtesy of having my phone calls returned."
- "He (she) hasn't returned one of my phone calls for the last two weeks. If he (she) doesn't call me today, tell him (her) not to bother because I will be getting a new lawyer."

HINT: *If you get angry at your lawyer, do not abuse the members of your lawyer's staff—it's not their fault. Besides, if you stay on their good side, believe me, they'll "go to bat" for you with their boss. But abuse them, and your message just might end up on the bottom of the pile.*

RIGHT #2

Clients have the right to receive copies of all important pleadings and correspondence

Clients commonly complain that they don't know what is happening with their own case. This problem can be substantially eliminated, if you direct your lawyer to send you copies of all important letters, pleadings and other documents as they are received or generated. While there may be a nominal charge made for the cost of copying voluminous documents, it is certainly well worth the price. When you receive your copies, be sure to read them carefully, and don't be afraid to ask questions about anything you don't understand.

HINT: *What I am urging you to do, in essence, is to keep a duplicate file of your own case. In order to keep control of the flow of paper work you will receive, it is important that you organize your file and keep it up to date. While I am sure you are capable of setting up your own system, I believe that the following will work well.*

Duplicate File Notebook

Go to any stationery store and purchase a three-ring loose–leaf notebook, a three-ring hole punch and a packet of tabs.

Label each tab as follows:
1. RETAINER AGREEMENT
2. MONTHLY BILLS
3. COURT DOCUMENTS
4. CORRESPONDENCE
5. EVIDENCE OR IMPORTANT DOCUMENTS
6. SUMMARY OF DISCUSSIONS WITH LAWYER
7. CALENDAR

As you receive a bill, or a copy of a letter your lawyer may have mailed on your behalf, or whatever, file it in the appropriate spot. In this way you will know what's happening (and what's not), and can otherwise stay on top of your case.

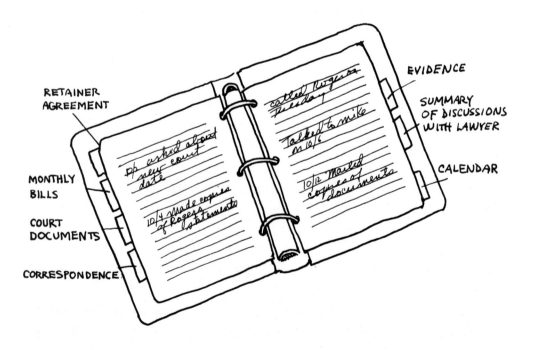

RIGHT #3

Clients have the right to a detailed monthly billing statement

When lawyers perform services such as making a phone call or preparing for trial, they charge the activity to the responsible client (you) so that they can get paid. Thus, by looking at his or her internal records, a lawyer can tell you what he or she did, when he or she did it and how long it took. You have the right to the same information!

Unfortunately, too many lawyers send bills to their clients which are confusing or which merely charge for "legal services rendered." So when you retain a lawyer, be sure to request a detailed monthly statement. And since there are many different billing systems used by lawyers throughout the country, it is also a good idea to ask your lawyer to show you a *sample bill* and explain it to you so that you will be sure you understand it. Following this procedure will also enhance your ability to monitor your own case and to keep fees within reason.

RIGHT #4

Clients have the right to have promises made to them kept

There is a vast difference between a lawyer knowing what to do and actually getting it done. So after you and your lawyer have agreed upon what action will be taken on your behalf, ask your lawyer *what* must be done to accomplish the task, *when* it will be done and *what* you can expect to happen next.

For example, suppose you and your lawyer have agreed you need to sue someone. The conversation could go something like this (remember, lawyers use words not used in everyday speech, so don't be afraid to ask about anything you don't understand):

> YOU: *"I've never sued someone before. What happens now?"*
> LAWYER: *"Well, I'll prepare a Complaint."*
> YOU: *"What's a 'Complaint'?"*
> LAWYER: *"It's a document that sets forth the facts of the case and why you believe you're entitled to damages."*
> YOU: *"How long do you expect that to take?"*
> LAWYER: *"I'd say a week."*
> YOU: *"I can expect the Complaint to be prepared by May 5th, then?"*
> LAWYER: *"Yes, barring the unforeseen."*
> YOU: *"Good. I'd like a copy of that when it's ready, please."*
> LAWYER: *"Okay."*
> YOU: *"After the Complaint is prepared, what happens next?"*
> LAWYER: *"We'll have you come in to read and verify it."*
> YOU: *"What do you mean, 'verify'?"*
> LAWYER: *"To sign it under penalty of perjury."*
> ETC.

So, using a simple question and answer format, you will have learned *what* specific action the lawyer will perform, *when* it will be performed, and *what* happens next. (You would be sure to file your notes in your Duplicate File Notebook, and mark May 5th on the calendar as the date the Complaint is due to be prepared.)

HINT: *In our example, the promise made by the lawyer to you was to have the Complaint prepared by May 5th. If you had not heard from your lawyer by May 7th that the Complaint had been prepared, you would have called your lawyer to find out why. If broken promises become habit you are not receiving the service you deserve (and are paying for). Schedule an office conference to find out why!*

RIGHT #5

Clients have the right to the truth, even if it hurts

When you hire a lawyer, one of the services that *you pay for* is a more objective, less emotional point of view than your own (or that of someone close to you). In order to be objective, your lawyer must look at *all sides* of the case—yours and your opponent's. After all, if your lawyer only looks at the case in the way you see it, he or she will not be able to anticipate problems and prepare to overcome them; that could lead to disaster! Also, good decision-making depends upon every aspect of the case being taken into consideration. For example, when discussing a settlement, the following could occur (note the difference in the following scenarios).

Scenario 1

LAWYER: *"Your opponent just made an offer of settlement of $15,000. I have to let his lawyer know our answer by the end of the day."*

CLIENT: *"What do you think?"*

LAWYER: *"Forget it! We're gonna win this case and make $30,000!"*

Scenario 2

LAWYER: *"Your opponent just made an offer of set-tlement of $15,000. I have to let his law-yer know our answer by the end of the day."*

CLIENT: *"What do you think?"*

LAWYER: *"It's a little low. If we win the case, we'll win $30,000. We've got a problem with their witness, though. If the jury believes her story, the whole case could go up in smoke."*

CLIENT: *"But she's lying!"*

LAWYER: *"The jury might not see that. She sure looked good at her deposition, and if you lose, you may end up owing them money for court costs.*

CLIENT: *"What do you recommend?"*

LAWYER: *"Well, there's a gamble in any trial—and $15,000 is a lot of money, but I think we can do better. What if we make a counter proposal that they pay $22,000? If they won't, you can always take the $15,000, but I vote we go to trial. It's up to you."*

Do you see the difference? In Scenario Two you are being given the full picture, the *"ups" as well as the "downs"*—with the situation as your lawyer sees it—including options, which makes it easier for *you*, the client, to make an intelligent decision.

HINT: *Intelligent decision-making requires information, so the last thing you want in a lawyer is a "yes man." As you discuss your situation with your lawyer, take note as to whether he or she discusses the "down side." If he or she doesn't, BEWARE! Something may have been missed!*

If you feel your lawyer hasn't given you the complete picture, don't ever be afraid to *ask.* Your conversation might go something like this:

CLIENT: *"Wow, things look good, don't they?"*
LAWYER: *"They sure do."*
CLIENT: *"Can you think of any problems we haven't discussed?"*
LAWYER: *"Well, I guess a problem could occur if your witness fails to cooperate."*
CLIENT: *"How can we make sure that won't happen?"*
LAWYER: *"Why don't I give him a call?"*

I know I stated this before, but I believe it bears repeating—if your lawyer ever makes a guarantee of success, *get a second opinion.*

RIGHT #6

Clients have the right to their lawyer's best effort

This should go without saying, but some lawyers don't do their best for every client. Here are some warning signals that your lawyer isn't doing his or her best for you:

1. Repeated failures to get work done on time.
2. Chronic unreturned phone calls.
3. Handling several other clients' court appearances at the same time as yours. (There are exceptions to this. Some appearances require little effort, such as setting a date for trial. But if your lawyer is handling several different hearings or trials, your lawyer may have bitten off more than he or she can chew.)
4. Repeated requests to a court for continuances (delays in hearing date).

5. Chronic tardiness.
6. Unfamiliarity with your case.
7. Repeated *unanticipated* setbacks. In other words, your lawyer is constantly surprised by things that go wrong, the potential for which was never discussed with you.
8. The repeated use of less experienced associate lawyers without prior approval by you.
9. Chronic ill health of your lawyer.
10. When a lawyer seems more interested in telling you his or her personal problems, than he or she is in hearing yours.

RIGHT #7
Clients have the right to know what's going on

Basically, that's what this book is all about. Your case or other legal involvement is a very important part of your life, and you not only have the right to know what's happening, but it is your attorney's *ethical duty* to inform you.

Here are a few thoughts on the subject not extensively covered in other chapters:

- Anytime your opponent makes an offer of settlement, your attorney *must* tell you what it is before responding. Remember, it's *your choice* to accept or reject, not your lawyer's.

- Likewise, any offer or communication of substance made to the other side on your behalf must have your okay.

- Your attorney must tell you if he or she has a conflict of interest—that is, if he or she represents or has represented another client who has an interest in conflict with yours. Likewise, if the lawyer has a personal interest in conflict with you, you must be notified.

- Your lawyer should tell you if other professional responsibilities or personal commitments may hinder his or her performance on your behalf.

- If new laws or court decisions affect your case in any material way, you should be advised immediately.

- Your lawyer should advise you if other members of the law firm will be performing services on your case. For example, you may hire a senior partner, who may delegate some of the work to a less experienced associate or law clerk. As I have said, this is a common practice which can work well for you.

HINT: *It's a good idea to have the above agreed to ahead of time and in writing. That way there will be no misunderstandings.*

However, you should be advised ahead of time of the practice, and be charged *less* for the associate's time than you would by a more experienced lawyer. Also be sure the lawyer you hired bears the ultimate responsibility for your file.

Obviously, this list isn't all inclusive, but I think you get the idea.

RIGHT #8

Clients have the right to confidentiality

This is basic, for there can be no effective legal representation without confidentiality. It is so important, that it is usually enacted into a law (varying from state to state) called *Attorney-Client Privilege.* This law (with limited exceptions) makes it your lawyer's solemn duty to protect your confidentiality no matter what consequences he or she might face—even if it means going to jail.

Luckily, confidentiality is rarely a problem in attorney/client relationships. However, there are a few things you should know:

- The attorney-client privilege is *lost* if you speak in a non-confidential setting. That means if you bring a friend into a conference with you, the privilege does not apply and your attorney could be forced, under certain circumstances, to reveal what you said. So, when in doubt, meet with your lawyer alone.
- The attorney's support staff, i.e., secretaries and law clerks, owe each client the same duty. Thus, if a secretary ever tells you about another client's case, tell your lawyer! Because this staff person might be telling that other client all about you!
- If you sue your lawyer for malpractice, you may be giving up your right to confidentiality, as it relates to the lawyer's decisions regarding your case.
- If you have told your lawyer the truth in conference, and then lie on the witness stand under oath, your attorney must take steps to stop you from committing perjury, which could affect the right.
- The privilege is *yours*—you can waive it if you choose.

If you have any questions, ask your lawyer.

RIGHT #9

Clients have the right to have their attorney comply with the Canon of Ethics

All lawyers' ethical conduct is controlled by laws or Bar regulations commonly known as the "Canon of Ethics." Some of what has been discussed previously, such as confidentiality, can be found there. Here is a partial list of other ethical duties your lawyer owes you under those regulations.*

- To place money you give him or her (other than for fees), in a client trust fund, and to maintain it in such a way that his or her personal funds are never co-mingled with yours.
- To transfer your file to a new lawyer or to yourself promptly upon proper request, whether he or she has been paid or not.
- To not abandon you or your case without prior notice, and (in many cases) without the approval of a court.
- To avoid the appearance of wrongdoing as well as actual wrongdoing.
- To advise you if he or she has made a mistake which materially affects your case.

Again, this list is *not* all inclusive. If you have any questions, contact your State Bar Association.

Regulations may vary from state to state.

RIGHT #10

Clients have the right to be treated with respect

This should go without saying, but far too many clients I have talked to are made to feel like Rodney Dangerfield. Simple things spell respect, such as:

- A support staff and lawyer who know your name and treat you with courtesy.
- Lawyers who don't "talk down" to you.
- Prompt return of phone calls.
- Not being placed on hold for long periods of time.
- An understanding attitude that you may be under stress and strain.
- Clean and neat waiting rooms and offices.
- Being asked by a smoking lawyer whether smoke bothers you.
- Being advised ahead of time if there has been a change in plans.
- Your lawyer holding his or her phone calls during your conferences.

Don't forget, you are the source of your lawyer's income—*demand respect!*

4

THE FLIP SIDE
OF THE COIN
CLIENT RESPONSIBILITIES

When you hire a lawyer, you owe it to yourself to do all that you can to make your attorney's job as easy as possible. This is not too difficult if you obey the following rules; paramount for having a successful relationship with your lawyer.

TELL THE TRUTH, THE WHOLE TRUTH, AND NOTHING BUT THE TRUTH

Lying to your lawyer is like cheating at solitaire—you never really win. Your lawyer's ability to protect your interests depends absolutely upon the accuracy of the information you supply concerning your case. This is especially true if you are involved in a lawsuit, so don't forget, your opponent will have a lawyer too—and if there's one thing lawyers do well indeed, it's catching people in lies.

Here are just a few of the consequences that lying to—or witholding information from—your lawyer may create:

- Your lawyer may make a tactical error(s) he or she would not have made, had the complete truth been known.
- Your lawyer may have to expend great effort in "damage control" just trying to get the case back where it was before . . . and *you* have to *pay for it!*
- Your entire case may be destroyed.
- The enthusiasm your lawyer may have previously had toward you and your case may wane or completely fizzle out. This is because *lawyers hate to be lied to by their own clients*—and they feel humiliated when the client gets caught.
- Lying under oath is a serious crime called perjury. So don't do it. You could go to jail.

BE PREPARED

Whenever you call your lawyer, or request an office conference, be sure you are ready by *writing down ahead of time* the questions you want to ask, or the facts you wish to discuss. In this way you won't have to call back to ask a question or give information to your lawyer you forgot to mention before.

Suppose you are suing your ex-employer for firing you without cause (wrongful termination). You are meeting with your lawyer to discuss your former boss's possible testimony. Your notes would read something like this.

NOTES TO TELL MY LAWYER

About a year before I was fired, my boss and I had an argument about the Vietnam war. He's treated me like an enemy ever since.

Three months before I was fired, my sales territory was cut in half and given to someone else. My boss's secretary, Mary Gossip, told me he was trying to make me quit.

My boss accused me of laziness in front of four co-workers one month before I was fired. He said my sales were down, so obviously I wasn't working very hard. I was very embarrassed.

I was fired for missing one week of work. I was sick— my doctor, Dr. Wright Prescription, can prove it.

The day I was fired, my boss told me to "cheer up." He was sure I could get a job with Fidel Castro.

I have been told that three years ago, another salesman was fired because he had a bumper sticker on his car that my boss didn't like. There may be others.

QUESTIONS TO ASK MY LAWYER

I promised Mary Gossip that I would never tell anyone that she told me my boss wanted me to quit. Can I keep her name out of it?

Should I ask Mary Gossip to meet with you?

How can we find the names of other people the boss fired because he didn't like their politics?

This kind of preparation is especially important if you are complying with your lawyer's request for information. I have known a full day's work to be wasted because a client's "afterthought" changed what I had planned to do.

Besides, when you are prepared, your lawyer's time is spent more efficiently—which *saves you money.* Remember, each phone call you make to him or her—and that he or she makes to you—is charged to your account.

PAY YOUR LAWYER

This is simply a matter of integrity. When you hire a lawyer, you and he or she make an agreement (the Retainer Agreement)—one part of which is your promise to pay for services rendered.

Here are some of the consequences of failing to keep your promise:

- Your lawyer may ask you to take back your file and will sue you for money owed. Not only will this prove disastrous to your case, but it will multiply your legal troubles (and possibly affect your credit rating).
- Your lawyer may just stop doing the work that needs to be done. This isn't really ethical, but it happens all the time.
- Other clients may suffer because of your poor conduct. A common criticism aimed at lawyers is the size of the fee that lawyers ask for in advance (the retainer fee). Believe it or not, this practice is, at least in part, an act of self-defense against being "stiffed." And, just as shoplifters cause prices to be higher in stores, non-paying clients sometimes force lawyers to charge more for their services.

> **HINT:** *Many lawyers will accept monthly payments or credit cards. So, if you have a problem paying the fee in full, don't be afraid to try to work out a deal.*

> **HINT:** *If, for whatever reason, you find you can't pay your lawyer, don't keep silent about your problem. Rather, schedule an appointment right away. Most lawyers will stick by you when you are in financial difficulty if you are honest with them and are willing to take reasonable steps to protect the lawyer's fee.*

COMPLY PROMPTLY WITH YOUR LAWYER'S REQUESTS

Your lawyer cannot be expected to place any more importance on your case than you do. So make sure you have your priorities straight. If your lawyer asks you to supply information, or take some sort of action, do so promptly—even if it means missing the Super Bowl, or a vacation weekend in the country. Failure to do so can produce some of the following unpleasant consequences:

- Your lawyer may do a less competent job. Your lawyer is frequently working under a time limit (especially in lawsuits), and the last thing he or she needs is the stress of working overtime because of your laziness. Besides, as Benjamin Franklin said, "Haste makes waste."
- Your matters may be put on the "back burner" while your lawyer services another client's case—a client who gives the lawyer the support he or she deserves. There is nothing more frustrating than the experience of sensing your lawyer no longer cares.
- A time limit may be missed, creating damage control work for your lawyer—which he or she hates

and *you pay for.* Occasionally, the missed time limit in and of itself can cause you to lose the case.

- Your lawyer may lose a tactical advantage that was previously gained. I've seen more than one case lost when the momentum went to the other side because lazy clients simply did not supply what was needed.

> **HINT:** *If your lawyer makes a request of you, always ask* when *he or she wants it, and whether he or she is working on a time limit, and be sure to use your calendar to be certain you don't forget.*

AVOID EMOTIONALISM

Being a client, you are probably going to approach your case from an emotional base. This is natural and your lawyer is trained to deal with it. But it sure helps your lawyer to "separate the wheat from the chaff" if you keep your emotions to a minimum.

For example, if you are in a child custody fight (believe me, no cases get more emotional—except for will contests, which prove, if nothing else, that blood isn't always thicker than water) and your lawyer asks you, *"Why do you believe the children should live with you?"* It is not helpful to say, *"Because my 'ex' is nothing but a dirty, lousy, cheating—BLEEP—who is only after the kids because I want them."*

That answer is worthless. It doesn't provide a starting point for your lawyer to build on. Compare it with the following answer, in which feelings have been set aside for the moment, and an answer has been given containing factual information: *"Well, I really believe the kids will be better off with me. I have always spent more time with them and have been more involved in their lives. Besides, their father works a lot of overtime and is rarely home before 8:00 P.M."*

While this is a general statement, at least it gives your lawyer a *factual basis* for further inquiry. For example, the client could then be asked for *specific examples* of when he or she spent more time with their children. These specifics will in time become the factual building blocks from which the case will be built.

Do you see the difference?

BE PUNCTUAL

Frequently, you will be required by your lawyer to be in court, or at an office conference, at a specific time. *Don't be late.* At best you will have irritated all concerned (including the judge), and at worst, your court case could be taken off the docket.

Here are a few tips that will help you be on time:

- Get complete directions of where you are going ahead of time and write them down.
- Ask your lawyer how long it takes to get to the location from where you will be coming.
- Leave a half hour early, just in case. You can always get a cup of coffee if you arrive before the appointed time.
- If you are going to court, ask what floor the particular courtroom is on—or—agree to meet at an easily located place, such as the elevators or the court cafeteria. If you are going to an office building, you may want to agree to meet in the lobby.

- *Always* get a phone number of where you can call, in case something happens that will make you late.

TELL YOUR LAWYER HOW YOU FEEL

Usually if a client is unhappy with an attorney, the lawyer is the last to know. He or she should be the first! So, instead of complaining to the mailman that your lawyer has overcharged you, or hasn't done a good job, *schedule an appointment* with your lawyer and *clear the air!*

Now, I know many people shy away from personal confrontations, especially with lawyers, but keeping silent doesn't make the problems go away—in fact it usually makes them worse.

SHOW APPRECIATION

This may seem like a minor point, but lawyers *care* very much whether you think they are doing a good job. So, be sure to give your lawyer "strokes" when warranted. It won't cost you anything, and it will make your lawyer happy, increase his or her enthusiasm for your case, and thus make him or her that much better an advocate for you. Besides, sometimes it's the little things that count: a card, a thank you—even a bonus!

5

IT'S DEEPER THAN IT LOOKS
COSTS: THE HIDDEN EXPENSE OF LAWSUITS

Brace yourself, I've got bad news. Your lawyer isn't the only one who has a hand in your pocket. There are many others who will benefit because of your legal problems; ranging from bureaucrats to stenographers, process servers to private investigators. In fact, whole industries are just out there waiting in line to send you a bill. Payments to these individuals, entities or institutions are known as "costs." Payments to your lawyer for services rendered are known as "fees." As you will see, both can add up to a bitter pill to swallow.

THE NATURE OF COSTS

For our purposes, "costs" can be defined as "any expense incurred during the course of a lawsuit, other than payment to lawyers for services rendered." Some costs, such as "filing fees," are mandatory (though they can be waived under certain conditions). Others, such as payments to "expert" witnesses*, are optional though frequently indispensable. Many costs are expensive, and in many lawsuits, the total spent can add up to thousands of dollars.

A partial list of costs which can be incurred in a typical lawsuit include:

Filing fees

Yes, you must pay the court for the "privilege" of suing or being sued. The cost of filing a Complaint exceeds $100 in some states, with the cost of filing an Answer, defending yourself, usually a little less. But that is only the beginning . . .

Service of process

Under our judicial system, people have the right to be notified that they are being sued. Witnesses are also frequently "served" with subpoenas. Naturally, the person who physically accomplishes this act must be paid—*less* if they are a public servant, such as a U.S. marshal—*more* if they are private process servers who earn their living

A "professional" who is paid to give his or her opinion about the case.

in this sometimes dangerous fashion. In any event, the total expense for "service of process" can run into the hundreds of dollars, before a case is completed.

Witness fees

When a witness is compelled by subpoena to appear in a court or at a deposition, most states provide that the witness is to be compensated for the expense of appearing. The total paid in witness fees can also amount to hundreds of dollars (in large cases). Don't forget, *you* are responsible for these costs.

Expert witness fees

Some cases cannot be proved or defended without "experts" giving their opinion on the issues involved. Medical malpractice cases are typical of this phenomenon, where doctors are called upon to testify as to the standard of care rendered by their colleague who is being sued.* Expert witnesses, be they auto mechanics or psychiatrists, get paid not only for the time they spend testifying, but also for the time they spend reviewing the facts and circumstances of the case. Again, *you* pay them, and they don't come cheap.

HINT: *Ask your lawyer if you are entitled to be paid back for these costs if you win the case. If not, you may decide you will be "money ahead" to settle out of court.*

Depositions

In most civil suits, the day comes when your lawyer decides he or she must take the deposition (an oral statement given under oath) of the other party, or, as is

---

The motion picture The Verdict *illustrates the importance of expert witnesses nicely.*

frequently the case, of almost anyone who has knowledge of the facts of your case. Under such circumstances, you not only have to pay a witness fee, but the far greater cost of the deposition itself, which consists of paying for a court reporter to record and transcribe the proceedings. The bad news is that the total of deposition costs frequently runs over $1,000 (sometimes *well* over $1,000). The worse news is that most lawsuits *cannot* be effectively waged without at least one or two depositions being taken.

Costs of investigation

Some cases require the services of professionals, such as a private investigator who may interview witnesses, take photographs and otherwise give your lawyer information that can serve as the foundation of your case. Other professionals who might be hired (and who may later become your expert witnesses) include accountants, mechanical engineers, doctors or accident reconstruction experts, just to name a few. I'm sure it comes as no surprise that these professionals are paid for their services, and not from the lawyer's personal funds either.

More commonly, however, the investigation of the facts is conducted by the lawyer through various legal means, many of which involve the spending of money. For example, when your lawyer obtains copies of bank records, the bank charges a fee for the duplication, which, in turn, will be charged to your cost ledger.

Now, obviously this list is not complete, but, as you can see, the expenses of litigation involve far more than lawyer fees.

Lawyers, especially in "contingency fee" cases (see next chapter), will sometimes "advance" costs on your behalf. In other words, the lawyer pays the costs as they come up, and receives repayment from you, either on a monthly basis or at the end of the case.

HINT: *It is unethical for your lawyer to agree to foot the costs for you without repayment, so be sure you fully understand the arrangement you have made with your lawyer regarding these expenses.*

Some lawyers demand that you deposit funds with them in advance of incurring costs. This is absolutely proper *if* the funds are placed in the lawyer's *client trust account*. Under no circumstances is the lawyer permitted to co-mingle his or her personal funds with your money that is being held in trust for payment of costs.

If you win a lawsuit, your opponent will probably be ordered to pay your costs. That's the good news. The bad news is that if you lose, you will be ordered to pay your opponent's costs. Chances are, however, that your case will "settle," that is, be resolved before trial. Under such circumstances you are responsible for your own costs, so keep this in mind during settlement negotiations. Also, remember that not *every* expense you have incurred can be ordered repaid by the loser, should you win the case. Ask your lawyer for the specifics in your jurisdiction.

Cost control is as vital to the effective management of a lawsuit as it is to the profitable management of a business. Thus, you should work closely with your lawyer in determining which cost items are worth paying for and which are not. In no event should your lawyer incur an individual cost in excess of $250 without your prior approval. After all, it is *your* money.

Remember, the money you spend on a cost *does not* include the fee your lawyer charges for services rendered in connection with it. For example, when your lawyer takes a deposition, you pay for the deposition itself (the cost) *and,* if your lawyer is charging you by the hour, a *fee* for the time the lawyer spent taking the deposition.

QUESTIONS TO ASK YOUR LAWYER ABOUT COSTS

"What things will you be doing that will create cost expenses for me?"

Many of the actions your lawyer will be taking will incur a cost which must be paid. By finding out what your lawyer's plans are ahead of time, you can learn how he or she plans to pursue your case, and you can prepare yourself for the expenses which will naturally follow.

"What is your estimate of the costs I will have to incur during this lawsuit?"

As set forth in detail at the beginning of this chapter, costs are an expensive proposition, and must be taken into account when deciding how a lawsuit will be conducted.

"When do you think these costs will occur?"

Forewarned is forearmed. If you know a deposition will be taking place in four months, which will generate a cost of $450, you can save for it.

"Will you please get my consent before you incur a cost in excess of $250?"

The point of this question is not intended to handcuff your lawyer, but to ensure that you remain a vital part of the decision-making process of your case. Also, if you trust your lawyer, pay great heed to the advice given. Such a conversation might go something like this . . .

LAWYER: *"Hello, Jean? This is I.M. Tough."*
CLIENT: *"Hi. How's the case going?"*
LAWYER: *"Fine. That's what I'm calling about. I think we need to take the deposition of the witness to the accident. It might be a long one. I estimate the cost to be about $400."*
CLIENT: *"Why do you think it's necessary?"*
LAWYER: *"She's the key to the whole case. Without her testimony, it's your word against the driver who hit you. If she supports your story, I think we can achieve an early settlement."*

Do not tolerate the following kind of treatment . . .

LAWYER: *"Hi, Jean. This is Fast Talker. I'm taking the deposition of I. Ball Witness."*
CLIENT: *"Really. Why?"*
LAWYER: *"Because I think it's necessary."*
CLIENT: *"Why?"*
LAWYER: *"You wouldn't understand."*
CLIENT: *"How much will it cost?"*
LAWYER: *"What do you care? I'm advancing the money for you. Now can I go ahead or not?!"*

Of course, none of you would have hired this kind of lawyer in the first place . . . would you?

6

THE BOTTOM LINE, OR WHAT'S IT GONNA COST ME?
HOW LAWYERS GET PAID

I'm sure you've all heard the saying "There's no such thing as a free lunch." Well, except in rare circumstances, "There's no such thing as a free lawyer"* either. So it pays to know how lawyers get paid.

*Public defenders don't count. They're not free. We all pay for them with our hard-earned tax dollars.

As we have noted, the field of law is quite broad, and as a result, the methods by which lawyers charge for their services can vary widely. Generally, however, fees usually fall into three categories: the *contingency fee*, the *hourly rate*, and the *statutory fee*.

CONTINGENCY FEES

Now I am sure most of you have heard many horror stories about lawyers and contingency fees, and while it may be an exaggeration to say that when the client gets a wheelchair the attorney gets a Mercedes Benz, there is enough truth in this joke to justify caution when retaining a lawyer on a contingency basis. Contingency fee cases are usually limited to accident or medical malpractice cases where there is insurance available to pay damages. And the mechanism of this fee arrangement is really quite simple: Your lawyer does not charge an hourly fee, but instead receives a specified percentage of the total amount of money recovered on your behalf. In other words, if no money is collected, no fees are owed.

Possible dangers

On the face of it, this seems like a risk–free proposition for the client. But in law, as in life, things are not always as they appear, so remember the following *caveats*—that's lawyerese for warnings—when dealing with a contingency fee case.

- As noted in the previous chapter, you are responsible for the *costs* of your case, even if you don't ultimately pay a *fee*. And, since your costs can amount to thousands of dollars, *a lost contingency fee case is not free*. This is especially true if you are ordered to pay your opponent's costs after losing a trial. I have seen more than one person find themselves suddenly and very deeply in debt when they lost a contingency fee case. So, if your lawyer tells you your case is "marginal," look before you leap—the money you save may be your own.

- The percentage that lawyers charge for their services varies widely—usually from 25% to as high as 50%! So be sure to shop around! My personal belief is that no one should pay more than 33% before trial and 40% if the case goes to trial—the additional 7% being justified by the enormous effort a trial requires of your lawyer.
- Many lawyers charge one percentage prior to filing a lawsuit, and a larger percentage after filing. Well, I'm going to let you in on a little lawyer secret. Filing the lawsuit itself is usually one of the easiest functions your lawyer will perform on your behalf.

This is especially true in the area of personal injury litigation where the Complaints are frequently standard "fill in the blank" type forms. So, as far as I'm concerned, raising the lawyer's "cut of the take," based upon the mere act of filing a lawsuit, is nothing but a rip-off.

- Everyone knows somebody who knows someone else who has had a contingency fee case settle, only to receive a pittance while the lawyer and doctors got rich. How, you may ask, does such an apparent injustice occur?

Assume you have been injured in an automobile accident. You sue. During the course of the lawsuit, a doctor treats you. You don't have health insurance. The doctor, in turn, agrees to defer his or her fee until the case is over. (This is done by filing what is known as a "lien" on the case.) You settle for $100,000. (Pray that you are never injured so seriously that an insurance company is willing to part with $100,000!) Here is how the money would be divided:

TOTAL RECOVERY		$100,000
CHARGES MADE AGAINST TOTAL RECOVERY:		
1. LAWYER'S FEE (40%)		40,000
2. DOCTOR'S LIENS		15,000
3. HOSPITAL LIENS		6,000
4. PHYSICAL THERAPIST LIEN		2,000
5. REPAYMENT OF COSTS ADVANCED BY LAWYER		8,000
	TOTAL	$71,000
BALANCE TO CLIENT		$29,000

This really isn't as unfair as it may at first appear. Remember, you received substantial medical care without cost until the case was over. Also, your lawyer advanced thousands of dollars to finance the case. But it does illustrate the importance of cost control—and health insurance.

Benefits

Now, before you decide that contingency fees are nothing but a lawyer's "con game," let's take a look at the bright side—for there are substantial benefits for you in contingency fee arrangements.

Affordability—As I stated, most contingency cases are really waged against insurance companies, who have been known to spend as much money fighting a case as they would have had to spend to settle it at the outset. This means extra work for your lawyer, which you would have to pay for if your lawyer were charging you by the hour. However, under the contingency fee system, extra work becomes your lawyer's problem and not yours, since the fee is based on the recovery.

Lawyer Enthusiasm—The amount of fees your lawyer earns is directly proportionate to the money you receive. Thus, your lawyer's enthusiasm is likely to remain high in a contingency case (if the case is a good one). After all, if your lawyer does a slipshod job, he or she is hurting him- or herself as well as you.

Lawyer Honesty—Since, in contingency fee cases, your lawyer's payday is deferred until you collect, he or she is not likely to take a case that does not look promising. Thus, if you can't find a lawyer to take an accident case on a contingency basis, the chances are your case just isn't worth pursuing.

Advanced Costs—Lawyers who practice in the field of personal injury realize "you have to spend money to make money," and are more likely to advance costs than are "hourly fee" lawyers. This can be very helpful, especially if you are on a limited budget.

HINT: *Even if your lawyer is advancing costs on your behalf, keep actively involved in the decision-making process as to whether to incur costs. After all, it is your money that is being spent, and you will ultimately have to pay the bill.*

THE HOURLY RATE

Abraham Lincoln once said, "A lawyer's time and advice are his stock in trade." To a large degree that remains true today, although I believe that Mr. Lincoln would be shocked to hear that an average lawyer, in a large city, charges about $150 an hour (that's more than $2 per minute)! Many in fact, charge as much as $300 per hour (I don't even want to compute what that comes to per minute)! Unfortunately, this is the reality of the marketplace, so it is incumbent upon you, the consumer, to know what you are being charged for, and the billing abuses to guard against.

What gets billed

When you pay your lawyer by the hour, virtually every function that is performed on your behalf gets billed. (In one office I know of, there are over 200 functions on the computer billing list to choose from.) Now, everyone expects a lawyer to charge for office conferences, research and court appearances. But, it comes as quite a surprise to some when they are charged for items such as phone calls, travel time, and the taking of notes—which lawyers euphemistically label "memos to the file." I even know of one lawyer who tried to charge a client for "thinking about the case!" (He didn't get away with it, thank goodness.)

The following is just a partial list of what lawyers do that you can expect to be charged for (to keep track of what your lawyer is doing, you will need a detailed monthly billing summary):

- telephone calls to client, witnesses, adverse counsel, court personnel, etc.
- writing letters
- reading letters
- preparing pleadings
- reviewing pleadings
- preparing for deposition
- attending deposition
- reviewing deposition
- research

- court appearance
- memos to the file
- review of file
- prepare judgment
- conference with associate regarding file
- conference with client regarding file
- conference with adverse counsel regarding file
- conference with witness regarding file
- conference with investigator regarding file

And this is just the beginning . . .

Billing abuses to watch out for

Each of the functions I have just listed are legitimately billed to your ledger when they are performed as part of the work on your file. There are some lawyers, however, who make charges for items that I do not believe are proper.

Secretary Time—If you get charged for secretarial time (except in extraordinary circumstances), protest loudly and strongly! Your lawyer's hourly fee is computed in much the same way as a clothing store determines the price of a suit—the cost of overhead (the expenses of doing business) plus an additional sum which provides the margin of profit. Secretarial salary is as much a part of your lawyer's overhead as is the rent, and not even the shadiest lawyer would try to charge a client an additional fee for rent (I don't think). Anyway, the principle is the same.

Photocopying—Like secretarial time, photocopying is a part of your lawyer's overhead. So, when copies are made, whether for file purposes or to be sent to you, I don't believe you should be billed. There may be a few exceptions, such as the copying of voluminous documents.

The Cost of Parking—Many lawyers argue that they have a right to charge their clients for their parking fees. I disagree, especially since you *know* they will deduct parking as a legitimate business expense (which is what it is) from their own income tax.

Unfortunately, billing abuses by lawyers are not limited to improper charges which are easy to detect. Some lawyers pad their bills in much the same way as some butchers do when they put their thumb on the scale. Some abuses to watch out for:

Double Billing—Double billing usually occurs when a lawyer goes to court. What happens is this—if the court appearance is relatively simple (such as setting a date for trial), the lawyer will bring other work with him or her to do while waiting for the case to be called. *This is perfectly legitimate. What isn't legitimate* is to charge *the client the lawyer is representing in court* for the full amount of time he or she is there *and* to charge the person whose file was worked on while waiting. (A lawyer joke tells of how lawyers invented the thirty-six-hour day. This is one way it's done). So, if you are in court and notice your lawyer working on someone else's file, make sure you are not charged for that time.

The Use of Unreasonable "Minimum Billing Units"—What is a "minimum billing unit" (MBU), you ask? It is the shortest time unit that a lawyer bills to your file. Its legitimate purpose is to simplify billing.

For example: A three-minute and twenty-second telephone call will be rounded off to three minutes—so would a two-minute and forty-second phone call. Where the abuse comes in, in my opinion, (if it occurs) is when lawyers lengthen the time of their minimum billing unit, not to simplify billing, but to reap unearned benefits. Thus, while a three or six-minute MBU may be legitimate, a fifteen-minute MBU, in my view, is not! (This is another method by which a minority of lawyers create the thirty-six-hour day.)

Speeding Up the Clock—As with any profession, a small number of lawyers are simply dishonest. These lawyers spend twenty minutes performing a function, then charge for thirty minutes. Luckily, if you have carefully screened your lawyer prior to retaining him or her, your chances of running into a crook will be greatly reduced.

Flat Fee for Court Appearances—Some lawyers charge an hourly rate, unless they are in court, whereupon they charge a flat rate. For example, if a lawyer charges $150 per hour, he or she may charge $500 for a half-day in court and $1,000 for a full day.

Now, many of my colleagues will disagree, but I believe this is a billing abuse. Court appearances vary in length from two minutes to six hours. To charge a flat fee frequently raises the value of an hour in court to double or even triple the lawyer's hourly fee! You wouldn't tolerate that in a plumber—and you shouldn't agree to such a billing scheme with a lawyer.

What your bill should look like

In order for you to really know what you are being charged for, you must receive a detailed monthly billing statement—which contains, at minimum, the following information:

- the dates within which the bill applies
- the date the service was rendered
- the nature of the service rendered
- the time spent on each service rendered
- the amount billed for each service rendered
- the total amount billed for the month
- credits given for previous payments
- total amount owed—or—total credit remaining from previous payments
- the amount of costs incurred
- the nature of the cost expense (i.e. filing fee, deposition, etc.)

Here is a sample of what I mean. The format is mine, and your lawyer's will probably differ. The key is whether you receive the information you are entitled to.

Wesley J. Smith
Attorney at Law

CLIENT BILLING STATEMENT - FROM JUNE 1 (YEAR) TO JUNE 30 (YEAR)

CLIENT NAME: G.I.M. LUCKY

HOURLY RATE: $120.00 PER HOUR

M.B.U. (MINIMUM BILLING UNIT): 1/10 HOUR (6 MINUTES)

DATE	COST	SERVICE	TIME	FEE CHARGE
6/2/( )		TELEPHONE CALL OPPOSING COUNSEL	0.2 HR	$24.00
6/3/( )		TELEPHONE CALL CLIENT	0.1 HR	12.00
6/4/( )	JURY FEE	—	—	128.50
6/5/( )		PREPARE FOR TRIAL	1.0 HR	120.00
6/6/( )		ATTEND TRIAL	3.5 HR	420.00
6/7/( )		PREPARE ORDER	0.5 HR	60.00
6/10/( )		CONFER CLIENT	0.5 HR	60.00
6/12/( )		TELEPHONE CALL OPPOSING COUNSEL	0.1 HR	12.00
6/22/( )		LETTER CLIENT	0.1 HR	12.00
		TOTAL CHARGES FEES	6.0 HRS	$720.00
		TOTAL CHARGES COSTS		128.50
		TOTAL CHARGES FEES AND COSTS		848.50
		CREDITS		
6/14/( )		PAYMENT RECEIVED - THANK YOU		$240.00
		PREVIOUS CREDITS OR CHARGES		0
		BALANCE DUE - FEES AND COSTS		$608.50

HINT: *If you had deposited funds in your attorney's trust account, which were utilized during the month, this should also be noted in the monthly statement as a credit to your account. You should also receive an accounting on your money held in the trust account as it is spent.*

Bills such as this have several advantages for you, the consumer. One important benefit is that the bill tells you exactly what your lawyer has (or has not) been doing. Also, the detailed nature of the summary allows you to monitor the *costs* being spent on your behalf—not to mention the *fees* being charged to you. Finally, it will provide a written history of what transpired during your case, should you need to refer back to it for any reason.

Warning! Some lawyers send their clients statements reading "FEES FOR SERVICES RENDERED $750.00." You should not tolerate this kind of billing statement. After all, you wouldn't accept a check at a restaurant which read, "CHARGES FOR FOOD CONSUMED $120.00."

Also, some lawyers, usually in divorce or criminal cases, will ask for a single flat fee—for example "$1,500 for the whole thing." Be careful here. If the lawyer is able to complete the case quickly, you may end up paying more than a fair rate based upon an hourly fee. Worse, if the case takes longer than anticipated, a less than scrupulous lawyer may begin to cut corners, or "hit you up" for more dough. Whatever you do, if you agree to a flat fee, get it in writing.

STATUTORY FEES

There are some areas of law in which the way your lawyer gets paid is set forth in the law itself.

Workers' compensation

This area of law is concerned with on-the-job injuries. If a lawyer is required, most states provide that he or she will be paid out of the proceeds of the case, as ordered by a judge or referee. If you have a workers' compensation case, ask your lawyer the exact procedure in your jurisdiction.

Probate

Fees for probate (the process of paying bills and disposing of property of a person who has died) are usually based upon a percentage of the value of the estate being administered. Again, the amount your lawyer receives will vary from state to state, so ask the lawyer you retain exactly how this system works in your particular area.

Indigent criminal representation

All jurisdictions provide counsel for poor people accused of a crime. However, many provide that some of these expenses shall be reimbursed by the client on an "ability to pay" basis. Ask your lawyer if your jurisdiction has such a repayment procedure, and your responsibility under it.

PREVENTION OF BILLING ABUSES

When you retain a lawyer, it is important to remember that you are engaged in a business transaction, not a personal relationship. Thus, it is not an insult to your lawyer when you take steps to prevent billing mistakes or abuses.

Keep your own time diary

Every time you interact with your lawyer, make a note of the time it took, and write it down. Then, when your bill arrives, compare the length of time you wrote down, with the time billed. If there is a major difference (or a whole lot of minor differences), speak up.

Determine your lawyer's minimum billing unit (if any) in advance

As I stated earlier, some lawyers say that they charge a certain rate per hour, but then charge a minimum of fifteen minutes for each transaction billed, which has the effect (if not the purpose) of raising the actual hourly rate. I would not hire a lawyer who engaged in this practice.

HINT: *Check the Retainer Agreement to see if a minimum billing unit is to be utilized. If it is not specifically provided for in the Agreement, it is probably improper to use minimum billing units.*

Make sure you don't get charged for time spent by your lawyer on another case

If you are in court with your lawyer, and you observe him or her working on another client's file, *politely* discuss the matter and make sure time spent on *that client's case* is not billed to you.

Add up the time billed to make sure the total charge is accurate

In recent years, most lawyers have switched from book-keepers to computer billing. And, while it is often said that computers don't make mistakes, their owners do. So, double-check the arithmetic on your bill, just in case. If you find an error, point it out to your lawyer.

When in doubt, speak up!

If you receive your bill, and you find a charge that you just cannot believe, contact your lawyer immediately. A mistake may have been made. Typical of such errors are services charged to the wrong client, or a mistake in the time billed. For example, a 1.1 hour charge being read by the computer as an 11 hour charge.

Rest assured that ethical lawyers do not wish to overcharge you. So, if you ever have any question or doubt about your lawyer's billing procedure, don't be afraid to ask questions. The ulcer you prevent may be your own.

THE RETAINER AGREEMENT

Except for the most simple of legal transactions (such as the preparation of a will), your business relationship with your lawyer (what is expected of you and what is expected of him or her), should be set forth in what is known as the Retainer Agreement. *The Retainer Agreement is a written contract and can be enforced as one. So, read it carefully before you sign it!*

Here are some provisions you are likely to find in your Retainer Agreement:

The retainer fee

When you hire a lawyer on an hourly basis, you are usually asked to pay him or her a lump sum payment "up front," known as a "retainer fee." Not only does the amount of the retainer fee differ from lawyer to lawyer, but so do the terms.

Some retainer fees are known as "earned retainers." In other words, if you pay your lawyer a $750 earned retainer, the lawyer is entitled to keep the money even if you change your mind and choose not to proceed. Under such circumstances, most lawyers would refund your money, less the actual time they billed on an hourly basis. However, not all lawyers are so understanding. So, if you are in doubt about proceeding with your case, ask your lawyer his or her refund policy *before* you pay.

Some retainer fees are paid *in addition to* the hourly rate. For example, if you pay a $1,000 retainer fee, and are being charged $150 per hour, you start from zero when the lawyer commences work. You *want* a retainer fee which is *applied to the hourly rate* so that if you pay a $1,000 retainer fee and are being billed $100 an hour, you would have a credit of ten hours' work before you owed the lawyer more money. *Be sure to check the terms of the Agreement* to see which of the above situations you are being asked to agree to.

The amount of the retainer fee is frequently negotiable. If your lawyer asks for $1,000, don't be afraid to offer less money. The worst thing that can happen is that you will hear those famous words, "No way, José." However, few lawyers in hourly rate cases will commence work without at least some front money. (Usually because they have been stiffed in the past.)

Many lawyers accept credit cards. So, before you pay the last of your grocery money on a retainer fee, ask.

You are not required to pay a retainer fee in contingency fee cases. (Although you may be asked to pay money in advance to the lawyer's trust account, for latter payment of costs).

The fee arrangement itself

This is the heart of the Agreement, in which you and your lawyer agree, in writing, upon the terms under which your lawyer will be paid. If your lawyer will be working on an hourly basis, the amount charged per hour will be listed. If it is a contingency fee case, the percentage the lawyer will receive, out of the recovery, will be specified.

> **HINT:** *While many lawyers* will not *adjust their rates, especially in hourly fee cases,* some will—*especially if your case is a good one. So, it never hurts to try. Remember, there are a lot of lawyers out there who really want your business!*

Provisions for payment of costs

The Retainer Agreement will also specify that you, the client, are responsible for payment of costs. As with fees, the terms by which you are to pay these costs are frequently negotiable. Also, as noted in the discussion of costs in the last chapter, be sure your lawyer agrees in writing that he or she will not incur *an individual cost* in excess of $250 without your prior consent. Such a provision in the Retainer Agreement might be worded something like this:

> "(Lawyer's name) agrees that he (she) shall not incur any cost chargeable to (client's name) in excess of $250 without receiving said client's prior consent."

Monthly payments

Some lawyers will permit you to make small monthly payments on your total bill. If so, make sure the minimum monthly payment, which will be permitted under the Agreement, is specifically set forth in the Retainer Agreement.

Lawyer's liens

Many Retainer Agreements, especially in contingency fee cases, provide that the lawyer has a "lien" against your case to secure attorneys' fees (make sure they are paid). What this means is that your lawyer is entitled to deduct funds that are received by him or her on your behalf, to pay attorneys' fees before you get your money. This is how it works:

Assume you have settled a case for $10,000 and you owe your lawyer $6,000.

- The person or entity who owes the money sends a draft or check for $10,000 to your attorney, made out to *both* you and your lawyer.

- You sign the check.

- Your lawyer deposits the check in his or her attorney trust account.

- When the funds have been cleared by the bank for payment, your lawyer will write him- or herself a check for payment of the fee—a check to others who may have liens on the case—and a check to you for the balance.

This is absolutely proper *unless* your Agreement with your lawyer does not provide that you have to pay him or her out of the proceeds of the case.

> **HINT:** *A lawyer is not entitled to force you to make payments that he or she is not entitled to receive under the terms of the Retainer Agreement, by keeping money you are entitled to in an account and refusing to give it to you until you agree to pay your bill. If this happens to you, or if you find your lawyer has deposited your money in his or her trust account without your permission, demand your money! If your lawyer refuses, contact another lawyer for assistance, and your State Bar Association.*

Your lawyer's duties

Usually, the Retainer Agreement will include, in general terms, your lawyer's duties towards you. Don't be alarmed if *every* ethical duty your lawyer owes you is not detailed, for it is already codified in the Canon of Ethics.

Provision for payment of attorneys' fees in the event of breach of contract

In the Retainer Agreement, you will find a clause in which you agree to pay the expenses incurred by your lawyer if he or she has to sue you for not paying your fees pursuant to the terms of the Agreement. This provision is perfectly legal. However, most states provide that such language also applies to you. In other words, should you have a fee dispute* with your lawyer that goes to court, which *you win,* you may be able to force your lawyer to pay *your* attorney's fees incurred to defend the lawsuit. If you have the misfortune of facing such a circumstance, check with a lawyer in your jurisdiction to determine if the "attorney fees enforcement provision" also protects you.

Final thoughts on Retainer Agreements

- Be sure to read your Retainer Agreement fully, *before you sign it.*
- If you have a question as to the meaning of any term, ask for clarification before you sign it. It

*See supplement at end of book, regarding attorney/client fee arbitrations in your state.

might also be a good idea to have your lawyer put the meaning of a questioned term in writing, as an addendum to the Retainer Agreement itself.

- Ask for a copy of the Retainer Agreement and keep it for your own reference. This may help prevent future misunderstandings with your lawyer regarding fees.

- Remember, as a general rule, the terms written in a Retainer Agreement will have control *over* any oral representations or agreements you may reach with your lawyer. So, if you and your lawyer enter into an oral agreement, which changes or is not a part of the written Retainer Agreement, make sure it is also set forth in writing. If your lawyer refuses to do so, find out why! If in doubt, send a letter to the lawyer setting forth the oral agreement agreed upon, and *keep a copy* for your own records.

- *Never* hire a lawyer based on an oral agreement. Always make sure your arrangement is set forth in writing, even if it is a simple one-paragraph letter.

QUESTIONS TO ASK YOUR LAWYER

"Will you please show me a sample bill and explain it to me?"

The look of the monthly statement you receive from your own lawyer may be drastically different from the example given in this chapter. Also, the bill is likely to contain abbreviations—which stand for certain services being billed. For example, "telephone call to opposing councel" may appear as "T.C.O.C." on your bill.

Just make sure you understand the bill you will be receiving before you leave the lawyer's office.

"I can't afford a $1,000 retainer fee, will you accept $600?"
OR

"I think a 50% contingency fee is too much. Will you take 40%?"
You should not be afraid to negotiate reasonable terms with your lawyer. After all, it is a business transaction. And while it is true that many lawyers have a "take it or leave it" attitude—you shouldn't be afraid to "leave it." Believe me, there are a multitude of other capable and honest lawyers out there just waiting for your business.

"I don't understand what this term means in the Retainer Agreement. Will you explain it to me?"
As I emphasize throughout this book, when in doubt, ask! There are no such things as stupid questions—only timid clients.

"Do you have a minimum billing unit?"
As noted earlier in this chapter, many lawyers bill according to "units" of time, not minutes. Find out what your lawyer's is and make sure it is set forth in the Retainer Agreement.

"What do you estimate the total billing fee will be?"
Lawyers rarely know the exact amount that their services will cost in a lawsuit setting; there are just too many variables. But they can sometimes give

you a ballpark figure. If you find out later that your fees are exceeding the estimate, ask why. There's probably a good reason, but check just to be sure. On the other hand, if you are retaining a lawyer to perform a specific service, such as the drafting of a will, the lawyer should be able to tell you exactly what it will cost in advance.

"Will you reduce your fee if I accept this settlement?"

This question would not arise until the later stages of your case, but since it concerns fees, I have placed it here. As a case gets close to trial, settlement negotiations usually begin. In many situations, the amount offered or demanded is a disappointment, but because of "problems in the case," your lawyer may recommend that it be accepted. At this point—with your lawyer reluctant to go to trial—you may be able to get your lawyer to take a small reduction in fee as an incentive for you to take the settlement (especially in contingency fee cases). Don't be afraid to ask.

HINT: *I don't mean to imply that lawyers deserve to be paid less when things don't work out. I merely want to point out that lawyers will sometimes compromise their fee toward the goal of achieving an acceptable resolution of the case—which benefits you both; your case ends, and your lawyer can go on to fry other, more lucrative, fish.*

"Are the fees I pay tax deductible?"

In some circumstances, lawyers' fees are tax deductible, but not in others. Ask your lawyer ahead of time. Then, if any of the fees are deductible, have your lawyer give you whatever documentation you will require to back up your claim with the I.R.S. After all, if Uncle Sam wants to pay part of the bill, let him.

WORKIN' 9 TO 5 8 7

WHAT LAWYERS DO

To the prospective law student (and to every lawyer's mother), the "life of lawyering" is one filled with excitement and intrigue, where lawyers, cast as "white knights," defeat the forces of evil in dramatic courtroom confrontations. To the disgruntled client, lawyers may appear to be modern day "Blackbeards"—pirates in

Mercedes Benzs, who ravage the innocent and protect the guilty in order to fill their treasure chests with gold. In reality, both images miss the mark, a lawyer's job is much more—and much less—than it at first appears to be.

THE ADVERSARY SYSTEM

Lawyers ply their trade under the rules of a game known as the "adversary system." Here is a rough sketch of how the system works.

When people discover they have a legal problem, they usually retain a "hired gun," known as a lawyer. When a lawyer agrees to take a case, he or she becomes the "advocate" of the person being represented.

Because the lawyer is an advocate, he or she is not expected to "do justice" (unless he or she is a criminal prosecutor). No, the responsibility of a lawyer to his or her client is that of a "fiduciary." In other words, the position is one of the highest trust, with supreme loyalty owed exclusively *to the client* (except in extraordinary circumstances such as being told by the client that they are about to commit a crime).

If the legal problem is a lawsuit, both sides will generally have lawyers to act on their behalf. The lawyers engage in a "paper war," both seeking victory for their sides of the dispute. In much the same way that generals plan their war maneuvers, lawyers plot out a plan by which they marshal facts. Whether it is the negotiation of a contract or the preparation of a trust, each lawyer tries to exploit the strengths of his or her client's case, while limiting the damage caused by the weaknesses.

Just as the rules of real war between nations is governed by the Geneva Convention, the paper war between lawyers in a lawsuit is governed by the Canon of

Ethics and other rules and regulations. These rules control the way the "game" is played, including the conduct
of the hired guns.

If the matter involves a trial, the lawyers will try to
make their client's case look as strong as possible, and
the other side's case as weak as possible, using every
ethical means of persuasion at their command—
regardless of who may really be "right."

At the trial, an "impartial third party" (a jury in a jury
trial, or a judge in a court trial) will try to determine what
really happened from the evidence presented by both
sides. This is called a "finding of fact," which the court
then uses to base its Orders and Judgments on, as it
seeks to "do justice."

The theory behind the adversary system is that truth is
best discovered by having lawyers work exclusively for
different sides (rather than by having them conduct an
impartial investigation).

Supposedly, the competition which is thereby created
between the lawyers acts as a stimulus whereby both
sides leave no stone unturned and no closet unopened,
in their quest for victory—which (in theory) ultimately
leads to "truth, justice and the American way." Unfortunately, *I don't think it does,* for several reasons:

- All lawyers are *not* "created equal." Good cases can be (and are) *lost* by poor lawyers.
- A good lawyer can *prevent truth* from being learned—in fact, it is frequently unethical for him or her *not to.*
- The rich and powerful are frequently able to dominate, because they can afford to have their lawyers do things that the less powerful can't.
- Well, I'm beginning to hyperventilate here, so I'd better get off my soap box . . .

My opinions notwithstanding, the adversary system is the only game in town, so let's get to some specifics . . .

CIVIL LAWSUITS

Have you ever felt like "suing the bastards?" Well, if you ever do, you will be participating in that popular American sport known as the "civil suit." Civil suits come in all sizes and forms, ranging from an action against a dry cleaner who ruined a twenty-five-dollar sweater to a multimillion-dollar lawsuit against the asbestos industry for negligence; from a tenant seeking to force a landlord to kill roaches to a class action seeking to prevent racial discrimination. Civil suits do have one thing in common—they are not fun. In fact, they are usually frustrating, time-consuming and expensive endeavors, where even the winners often feel like losers. So, fasten your seatbelts, here we go . . .

The opening rounds

Civil suits usually begin when the party who is suing (known as the "plaintiff"), files a "pleading," known variously as a Complaint, Petition or Claim, with a court.

The purpose of the document is to let the person or entity being sued (usually known as the "defendant") know the facts and law upon which the case is based. The case is "filed" by depositing the Complaint with the court (along with filing fee). There, the court clerk gives the case a number, issues a "Summons," and enters it into the court's records. Copies of the Summons and Complaint are then given (served) to the defendant by a process server, the lawyer, by mail or otherwise as permitted by law.

If you want to sue, your lawyer's duties include:

- gathering the facts, (including discussions with experts and witnesses where applicable).
- deciding the legal grounds for the lawsuit, including researching the law if necessary.
- preparing the Complaint in a proper fashion.

- physically bringing the Complaint to the court for filing.

> **HINT:** *Most lawyers make use of businesses known as "attorney services," which file documents with a court for free. If you are charged for the act of filing a lawsuit, ask your lawyer if he or she uses an attorney service before you pay the bill.*

- seeing to it that the defendant(s) is properly and legally "served."

> **HINT:** *The attorney services make their money "serving process" and, while they may cost more than a U.S. marshal, they are usually more reliable.*

- making sure the defendant responds to the lawsuit.

The ball is now in the defendant's court. He or she may:

- ignore the case. Of course, that almost guarantees the plaintiff a victory.
- admit the plaintiff is right.

> **HINT:** *If you are sued, and the allegations of the Complaint are true (in other words, you owe the money), you may still wish to hire a lawyer to negotiate a settlement, or do so yourself. Plaintiffs will frequently take less money, or monthly payments, in order to avoid the frustrating problem of collecting money from somebody who doesn't want to pay.*

- file a "motion" in court, "attacking the pleading," that is, requesting a judge to void the Complaint (usually because it has been improperly prepared*). If the judge agrees, the plaintiff is almost always given another chance to prepare a proper Complaint.
- say (at the same time the Answer is filed), in effect, "Sue *me*, will you? Well, I'm not taking this lying down, so I'm suing *you* back—nyah, nyah, na nyah, nyah!" He or she does so by filing a "Cross Complaint" or a "Cross Claim." Then, the plaintiff becomes a defendant (usually called a "cross defendant") and the whole process repeats itself. Other parties can also be brought into the lawsuit at this time as cross defendants in turn become cross complainants. Sounds confusing, huh? I have seen a few cases where a lawsuit and counter lawsuits have become so complicated, even the lawyers had a hard time figuring out what was going on. (Ain't law fun?)

If you have been sued, your lawyer's duties include:

- gathering the facts of the case.
- deciding the legal validity of the Complaint, and conducting any research that may be necessary to do so.
- determining what defenses, if any, you have to the lawsuit or the Complaint.
- preparing and filing any attacks on the Complaint.
- preparing and filing an Answer.

This is a very technical area of law, with rules varying from jurisdiction to jurisdiction. If I just tried to summarize the ways a Complaint can be attacked, this book would begin to read like a Bar examination.

> **HINT:** *When you are sued, the Summons will tell you the time you have within which to file an Answer with the court. If you miss this date, the plaintiff's lawyer may file a document in court called a "Default," which will permit the plaintiff to pursue the case "without your voice being heard." If you find that your time is running out, and you haven't hired a lawyer, call the plaintiff's lawyer and ask for an "extension of time within which to Answer." If he or she agrees, confirm the fact with a letter to the attorney. (Be sure to keep a copy of the letter for your own records).*

- preparing and filing any counter lawsuits that may be appropriate.

> **HINT:** *If counter lawsuits are going to be filed, they should be filed at the same time the Answer is. Otherwise you may have to ask permission of the Court to file them.*

Trench warfare

At some point, these initial skirmishes come to an end, and the lawsuit enters a new phase known as "discovery." The purpose of discovery is for all parties to learn everything they can about the other side and their own case (on the theory that knowledge promotes settlements). The name of the game here is *tedium*. Here is a partial list of the "tools of the trade."

Depositions

A deposition occurs when a lawyer for one side compels a party or a witness to submit to questioning under oath in front of a court reporter, who records everything that is said. The other parties then have a right to cross-examine the witness. The process is similar to being in court, with one major difference—there is no judge to keep the peace—and if the lawyers have strong personalities, things can threaten to get out of hand (in very rare cases, punches have even been thrown).

I cannot overstate the importance of depositions!
They are, in my view, the heart of any case. Why? For several reasons.

- Depositions are conducted with the witnesses taking the same oath they take in a court of law. In other words, lying in a deposition is the same as lying in court—it's a felony (crime) called perjury.

- The depositions are recorded and transcribed into a booklet, which has the effect of setting the testimony given down in concrete. Subsequent changes in testimony may be commented on at trial—which can destroy a witness's credibility.
- Lawyers use depositions to poke and prod at the opposition's case. Flaws that are discovered will be fully exploited, both during the discovery procedures and at trial.
- The facts gathered at a deposition define the case for the lawyers—allowing them to judge the strengths and weaknesses of the case.
- Lawyers also judge the way the witness "looks," and make a determination of whether a judge or jury will "like" the witness, or "believe" what the witness says (regardless of whether it is the truth).
- Settlement negotiations and trial strategy are based in a large part on the outcome of depositions.

IF YOUR DEPOSITION IS GOING TO BE TAKEN, I CANNOT OVEREMPHASIZE THE IMPORTANCE OF PREPARING FOR IT IN ADVANCE WITH YOUR LAWYER! UNDER NO CIRCUMSTANCES (IF YOU ARE A PARTY TO THE LAWSUIT), SHOULD YOU WALK INTO A DEPOSITION "COLD." If you do, (to paraphrase Bogart) you will probably regret it, ". . . maybe not today, maybe not tomorrow, but soon and for the rest of your case."

Interrogatories

Interrogatories are written questions which must be answered *in writing,* under *oath,* and boy, are they a pain in the . . . uh, neck! (Wait until you receive a two-inch-thick set of interrogatories containing five-hundred questions, and you'll know what I mean.) The questions run the gamut from requesting personal information to asking the names of witnesses, to describing your version of the facts of the case. When you answer interrogatories *be sure to be accurate,* as any errors will be exploited fully—and sometimes unfairly—by the opposition. (War is indeed hell—so are lawsuits.)

Document subpoenas

In the "search for truth," lawyers will also obtain copies of whatever documentation (bank records, medical reports, etc.) that are relevant to the case. (Just be thankful *you* don't have to review the reams of paper that can be generated in this way.) Lawyers use the documents they obtain as direct evidence, or to refute (or support) the testimony of the witnesses in a deposition or at trial.

HINT: *As you can see, when you are a party to a lawsuit, you lose substantial amounts of your privacy. So, if you have anything to hide, tell your lawyer ahead of time. What your lawyer* doesn't know can hurt you!

Motions

As I am sure you can well imagine, there are frequently substantial disagreements that occur during the discovery phase of lawsuits. These disagreements are resolved by going to court in a process known as a "motion" and letting a judge decide who is right.

HINT: *If a party refuses to meet his or her obligation to provide discovery, that party can have what is known as "sanctions" ordered against it. Sanctions are usually orders compelling one side to pay the other side money. In serious cases, a judge can actually enter a Judgment in the case against a party, and in extreme cases, order a person jailed for contempt of court!*

Your lawyer's duties during discovery include:

- knowing where to look for information, and which discovery "tool" to use.

- determining, with you, how much discovery should be done.

HINT: *Remember, when you engage in discovery, you usually incur costs (not to mention fees), so you and your lawyer should decide how to proceed using a "cost versus benefit" approach. In other words, is the money you will spend worth the information you will receive? Also, the extent of the discovery should be defined by what is at stake. For example, spending $5,000 may be too much in an $8,000 lawsuit, but not enough in a $100,000 lawsuit.*

- attending every deposition that is held. This is vital! If your lawyer misses a deposition, your point of view will not be represented.
- protecting you from "discovery abuses."

> **HINT:** *Sometimes lawyers get carried away and turn a civilized lawsuit into The Crusades. At such times, abusive, irrelevant and harassing tactics may be employed. It is your lawyer's job to stop such behavior in its tracks!*

- keeping the information obtained filed in an organized manner.

> **HINT:** *Discovery does no good if the information gathered is lost. Think of your lawyer as building your case like a child sets alphabet blocks in a row to form words. If you find the letter "I" and lose it, you will never be able to spell "WIN!"*

Peace talks

At some point in the lawsuit, the lawyers begin talking "settlement"—in other words, they try to fashion an ending acceptable to everyone so that a trial can be avoided. These talks sometimes begin before the lawsuit is even filed, and usually occur as each new fact is disclosed during discovery (a process which, by the way, can take years).

If, as the time for trial approaches, the lawyers and parties have not resolved the dispute, they are frequently given a helping hand by the court in a hearing usually called a "mandatory settlement conference." The conference is usually held in private, in the judge's chambers (office). During the conference, each lawyer tries to "sell" his or her side of the case to the judge. Ultimately, the judge gives his or her recommendation as to how the case should be settled. Most cases are resolved either before, or at, the settlement conference.

> **HINT:** *This settlement conference is not a trial, and you cannot be compelled to accept the judge's recommendation. But, before you refuse— think twice—because the judge's thoughts reflect the opinion of a knowledgeable and objective third party.*

Your lawyer's duties regarding settlement and settlement conferences include:

- having a detailed knowledge of your case—both its strengths and weaknesses.
- effectively communicating these strengths and weaknesses to you.

> **HINT:** *Do not be angry with your lawyer when he or she points out the weaknesses of your case. That's an important part of your lawyer's job. And, if he or she is good, your lawyer will be sure to hide his or her feelings from the opposition.*

I remember one case that I *knew* my client would lose, and I told him so. I was instructed to "settle for what I could." I decided to bluff the opposition by demanding we go to trial! They must have thought I knew something they didn't (or maybe they knew something I didn't) because we got a very good settlement. I tell you this "war story" so that you can see how lawyers sometimes act one way with the opposition, and another way with you.

- giving you his or her recommendation regarding the settlement.

> **HINT:** *Although the decision is yours, and yours alone, pay close attention to your lawyer's feelings. After all, recommendations are part of what you are paying for. Just be sure that you fully understand the reasons for the recommendations and the ramifications which will result before you decide.*

- making sure all of the "i"s are dotted and the "t"s are crossed. In other words, your lawyer should make sure that every issue raised in the lawsuit has been resolved, otherwise the settlement may fall apart—or worse—you could receive the burden of a settlement, but miss the benefits.
- making sure all of the necessary paper work is prepared in a proper and timely fashion.

Armageddon

If the parties do not settle, they go to trial. The game here could be called "Win or Lose," "Triumph or Tragedy," "Life or Death," (well, you get the point). And while trials can result in a verdict which finds the middle ground, usually one party winds up happy and the other sad (except in divorces, where both parties usually end up mad). Thus, a trial is usually a tense, all-consuming effort. (Your lawyer may work as long as fourteen or sixteen hours a day. You probably won't get much sleep either.)

Your lawyer's responsibilities at trial include:

- knowing the facts and law of your case—"*cold.*"

HINT: *How do you spell "successful trial?" P.R.E.P.A.R.E.! Not only at the time of trial—but during the whole discovery phase of the lawsuit. Nothing feels worse than losing a case because of a surprise.*

- having the skills necessary to effectively conduct a trial.

HINT: *I frequently talk to friends who have served on juries, and am appalled at how often they criticize one lawyer or the other as being an "embarrassment" or a "lousy lawyer," because they were doing a "bad" job for their client. So, make sure your attorney knows his or her business. (One way to find out is to ask your lawyer to allow you to watch him or her in action, then you can see for yourself.)*

- preparing you for your part at the trial.

HINT: *This not only includes rehearsing your testimony (practicing in advance), but letting you know how to dress and how to behave while you watch the proceedings. Remember, you are being watched even when you are not on the witness stand.*

- making sure all of your witnesses appear on time and are "rehearsed."
- making sure all of the documents to be introduced at trial are ready to go.

After the ball is over

At the end of the trial, a verdict is reached whereby the court issues orders in a document usually known as a Judgment. After the judge has signed it, the Judgment is entered in the court records and becomes binding on the parties—unless it is "stayed" (suspended) by some reason, such as an Appeal.

Notes to the winner

Just because you win the case, it doesn't necessarily mean that you will receive all of the fruits of victory. If the defendant refuses to, or can't, comply with the terms of the Judgment, you may have to "enforce" the orders of the court—that is, seek the assistance of the court or other appropriate government agencies in forcing the loser to comply with his or her responsibilities. Enforcement can be a very tricky and frustrating business, and it is not every attorney's strong suit, so make sure your attorney is up to the task. If he or she is not, you may wish to retain new counsel. Also make sure your attorney files the document necessary to collect your costs. Sometimes they forget.

If you are the winner, your lawyer's responsibilities after the trial include:

- preparing the Judgment to be signed by the judge.
- filing the documents necessary to make sure you can collect your costs from the loser.
- arranging with the loser's lawyer for the loser to comply with the orders of the court.
- advising you of the terms of the Judgment.
- defending the Judgment against post-trial attacks.

HINT: *There are a lot of things a loser can do to try to alter or delay your fruits of victory. Your lawyer's job includes resisting these efforts.*

- enforcing the Judgment if the loser refuses to comply with its terms.

Notes to the loser

Losing never feels good—but things aren't necessarily over. (Some lawsuits seem to have a life of their own.) If you feel strongly that the court has "done you wrong," you can always Appeal. (For that matter, so can the winner, who feels he or she has not won "enough.") But, even if you don't appeal, there are things you can do, ranging from filing a motion for a new trial to filing bankruptcy—things that can lead to your "rising like a Phoenix from the ashes." Consult your attorney for specifics.

If you are the loser, your lawyer's responsibilities after trial include:

- making sure the terms of the Judgment prepared by the winner are accurate.

> **HINT:** *I have heard of lawyers trying to get more from a Judgment than was given to them at trial. If this is attempted, it is your lawyer's job to stop it.*

- making sure that the winner's claim for costs is accurate.

> **HINT:** *Not all costs are recoverable from the loser. So, you don't want to pay more than you legally owe.*

- advising you on whether to comply with the Judgment or resist it by way of post-Judgment proceedings, such as a request for a new trial.
- preparing post-Judgment attacks in a proper fashion and filing them with the court "on time." (There is usually a time limit.)
- advising you of your responsibilities under the Judgment. And what, if anything, you can do to soften the blow.
- advising you of whether the case is worth appealing.

> **HINT:** *Appeals are very hard to win. So, unless a lot is at stake, or there were some terrible mistakes made at trial, or you feel very strongly about the outcome, you probably will not want to Appeal.*

CRIMINAL CASES

If you ever have the misfortune of being accused of a crime, you will know how Dorothy felt when she was hit by a tornado and transported to the Land of Oz. Nothing in your life will ever be the same. And, if you ever want to get back home again, it is going to take a lot more than a pair of ruby slippers; it's going to take hard work and a good lawyer!

Picking a good lawyer

Your choice of a lawyer is probably the most important decision you will make during your stay in Oz. So, don't choose your companion as Dorothy did hers—by chance. Make sure your lawyer is a skilled and experienced advocate. Remember, the prosecutor will be a dedicated professional, who, unlike the Wicked Witch of the West, will definitely *not* melt. And he or she *will* be after you!

HINT: *As a general rule, try to use a local lawyer for a locally charged crime, because he or she is more likely to know the terrain, i.e., the prejudices and personalities of prosecutors, judges and local police officials. For example, a friend of mine practices exclusively in the criminal field. He tells of a case in which a battered wife was accused of murdering her husband. He knew that one local judge hated abusive husbands, so he delayed the case until that particular judge was free to conduct the trial. He then "waived jury," letting the judge decide guilt or innocence. His client was acquitted (found innocent). A lawyer who didn't know about this judge's "buttons" might not have done as well.*

The investigation and arrest

When a crime has been committed, the police and other law enforcement authorities begin to investigate the crime with the intention of bringing the guilty to justice. When they think they have enough evidence, the arrest occurs. Bail is set and a time established for the suspect (called "the defendant") to enter a plea of "guilty" or "not guilty."

HINT: *If you are suspected of having committed a crime, consult a lawyer immediately! The fact that you may be innocent should not deter you. Justice does not always prevail. And remember, if you are arrested and cannot afford a lawyer, speak up! One will be provided for you!*

Your lawyer's responsibilities during the initial investigation and arrest include:

- advising you of how to conduct yourself during the investigation and making sure your Constitutional rights are protected.
- being present if you agree to be questioned, to make sure it is done properly.
- negotiating your surrender if you are to be arrested.

HINT: *The legality of an "arrest" depends on whether the authorities have acted within the Constitution and the laws of the jurisdiction in which the arrest occurs. So, be sure to tell your lawyer all of the facts and circumstances you can remember about the arrest. It may be important.*

- referring you to a reputable bail bondsman so that you can be released from jail on bail.
- meeting with you to determine your side of the story.
- reviewing the Police Report or other statements which may be available.

The arraignment

At the arraignment you either plead "guilty," "not guilty" or "no contest." The amount of bail is reviewed and sometimes "plea bargains" are worked out, resolving the case in its entirety. A date is *also* set for further hearings, or trial (as the case may be).

Your lawyer's responsibilities at the arraignment include:

- obtaining the Police Report, if it has not already been made available.
- advising you whether to plead "guilty" or "not guilty." Some cases are not worth fighting. At such times, you may wish to plead "guilty" or work out a deal. But *never* do so without at least talking to a lawyer first, because the consequences can go far deeper than you think.
- arguing to have your bail set as low as possible. Or, if you have a "clean record" and are well-known in the community, you may be eligible to be released on your own recognizance (an "O.R. release"). Ask your lawyer if you qualify.
- if appropriate, trying to have your case removed

from the criminal justice system. Some jurisdictions have programs (usually called "diversion") which will take a defendant out of the criminal justice system and put him or her into a counseling program (usually if the arrest is concerned with drug or alcohol abuse). Ask your lawyer if your jurisdiction has such a program, and if you qualify.

- obtaining jail house services. If you must remain in jail, your lawyer may be able to get court orders which will make that hardship a little easier to handle. Simple things, such as a haircut, medical treatment or telephone calls, can mean a lot when you are incarcerated (jailed).
- plea bargaining. Sometimes prosecutors can be convinced to reduce the charge in return for a guilty plea.

HINT: *If you ever plea bargain, be sure to get a complete picture of the consequences from your lawyer—both short- and long-term. For example, if you are an alien, your plea bargain might get you off with a small fine, but later, it could also get you deported!*

Pre-trial Proceedings

Before you get to The Land of Oz, you must walk through "dark forests" and "magical poppy fields" of pre-trial proceedings. Whatever you do, don't fall asleep! You may wake up in prison! During this period before trial, your lawyer may engage in one or more of the following:

Discovery motions
Discovery in criminal cases is not as complicated as in civil cases. There are no depositions, no interrogatories, and (except in Federal Court) usually only one party is

entitled to engage in it—the defendant. In "criminal discovery," the defense attorney receives from the prosecutor all of the information (with certain exceptions) known to the prosecutor, whether it hurts or helps the prosecutor's case.

Your lawyer's responsibilities at these proceedings include:

- knowing what information to ask for. The requests for information generally need to be specific in nature, so your lawyer should do his or her homework ahead of time.
- filing the motion in a timely fashion.

HINT: *If you will be having a preliminary hearing, your lawyer will want all the information the prosecutor has in his or her possession beforehand. After all, the more your lawyer knows ahead of time, the better he or she will do at the hearing.*

- fighting in court for information the prosecutor does not wish to divulge.

While many discovery motions are routine, not all of them are. Sometimes, there is a heated dispute over what information you are entitled to receive. Your lawyer must be ready to fight, which means he or she must not only have detailed knowledge of the reason for requesting the information, but also a thorough grasp of the law which supports his or her right to make the request.

Motions to exclude evidence

If your lawyer believes that the police or the governmental authority obtained evidence against you illegally—in other words, they violated your Constitutional rights—your lawyer requests a hearing where the judge is asked to throw out the evidence illegally obtained. If the evidence is thrown out, it can't be used against you. If enough evidence is "lost" in this way, your lawyer may get the case dismissed. This is the domain of the famous "legal technicality."

Your lawyer's responsibilities in such motions include:

- having detailed knowledge of the facts which give rise to the claim of illegal police conduct. Consequently, your lawyer should ask you all of the details surrounding your arrest(s), and the circumstances under which you may have made incriminating statements. If he or she doesn't, find out why.
- possessing a detailed knowledge of the type of law involved.

HINT: *If you are charged with a crime, especially if it is a serious one, the lawyer you select should really practice exclusively in the field of criminal law. One reason is this: the laws surrounding confessions, search and seizures, and other Constitutional issues are in a state of constant change. Only persons who devote their careers to the field can possibly keep up.*

- being prepared for a court hearing, including preparing you to testify (if that will be necessary), and being ready to conduct an effective cross-examination of the police or other governmental authorities who may have violated your rights. Your lawyer must also draft a written legal brief for the judge's use at the hearing.

Preliminary hearing

In most states, you are entitled to a preliminary hearing if you are charged with a serious crime. The hearing is held before a judge who determines whether there is enough evidence to justify a formal trial. (If there isn't, the case is dismissed). Your lawyer can use the hearing like a civil lawyer does a deposition.

Your lawyer's responsibilities at a preliminary hearing include:

- understanding the facts and law surrounding your case so that he or she can effectively "cross-examine" witnesses against you, thus making an effective "record" (a court reporter will be taking everything down).

HINT: *Don't be surprised if your lawyer doesn't permit you to testify. After all, he or she doesn't want the prosecutor to make an effective record against you.*

- being ready to plea bargain if it is appropriate to do so.
- obtaining orders for jail house services, if needed.

Pre-trial hearing

Pre-trial hearings are the swap meets of the criminal justice system. Their purpose is to settle cases before trial, and frequently the best deals are available to you here.

Your lawyer's responsibilities at a pre-trial hearing include:

- having a detailed knowledge of the strengths and weaknesses of your case, so he or she can convince the prosecutor to reduce or drop the charge, or agree to a reduced punishment.

HINT: *A good criminal lawyer has such broad knowledge of the law that he or she can often convince a prosecutor to allow you to plead guilty to a different, but less serious crime, in exchange for a dismissal of the crime originally charged. For example, if you are charged with "petty theft" arising out of a shoplifting episode, a good lawyer might be able to convince a prosecutor to allow you to admit to the crime of "trespass."*

- being able to explain to you the short- and long-term consequences of pleading guilty to a crime.
- discussing your prospects with you should you turn down a plea bargain and decide to go to trial.

Trial

This is the end of the yellow brick road. By now, the prosecutor has conducted his or her investigation, interviewed the witnesses that will be called against you, and has a general idea of what he or she will do at trial. So should your lawyer.

Your lawyer's responsibilities at trial include:

- having a detailed knowledge of the facts and law of your case.

- having prepared "jury instructions" which he or she will ask a judge to give to the jury. Before the jury is allowed to make its decision, they receive instructions on the law from the judge. The wording of these "instructions" can have a significant impact on "innocence" or "guilt." So, both the prosecutor and your lawyer will be working hard to get the judge to use language they like.
- making sure that your witnesses are in court and ready to testify when the time comes.
- preparing you for your testimony, should you decide to do so.

HINT: *You cannot be compelled to testify. And, for tactical reasons, your attorney may choose not to put you on the stand. Such a move is risky, but it can work—just ask John DeLorean!*

Post-trial proceedings

If you are found *not guilty*, it's all over (except for the bill). Break out the champagne! (You might even consider treating your lawyer to dinner.) However, if you are found *guilty*, some of the most important work your lawyer does for you will begin.

Among your lawyer's responsibilities to you after trial are:

- working with the court investigator or Probation Department to see if they will recommend alternative punishment or a reduced jail sentence.

After a person is found guilty of a crime, an investigation is conducted into the matter by the Probation Department or other investigating agencies before sentence is pronounced. Your lawyer should be in contact with them to see if they will support probation or community service instead of jail—or at the very least a reduced jail sentence.

- trying to convince the judge not to put you in jail, or to reduce your sentence.
- making a motion for a new trial if there were serious errors in the original proceeding.
- requesting that you be permitted to remain free on bail, pending the Probation Report or an Appeal.
- protecting your right to Appeal.

HINT: *If an Appeal is to be undertaken, most states require that certain action be taken on the Appeal within a specified time. Make sure you ask your lawyer to take the action, even if you will be using a different lawyer for the Appeal. Otherwise, you could find yourself "up the conviction creek without an Appeal 'paddle.' "*

APPEALS

When the smoke has cleared after a trial—be it civil or criminal in nature—one side or the other generally figures out that they lost, and looks around for ways to snatch victory out of the jaws of defeat. Many turn to the Appeal.

An Appeal is a lengthy, expensive and time-consuming process where a higher court reviews what occurred at "the trial court," to see if any mistakes have been made. If there were mistakes, and those mistakes were substantial, they may reverse the case and order a new trial, or take other actions to "right the wrong."

However, if mistakes were made (which usually happens), but those mistakes are deemed "harmless," the trial court's actions will be "affirmed" or allowed to remain in effect (under the theory of "no harm, no foul"). By far, more cases are affirmed than reversed.

Basically, here's what happens:

- One side or the other files a Notice of Appeal or other court document which serves to alert the court and the other side that an Appeal is to be taken.
- The official record of the case is ordered and sent to the Appellate Court.

HINT: *In civil cases, the preparation of the record costs* a lot of money. *If you win, the court may order these "costs on Appeal" repaid to you by the loser. Of course if you are the loser, you may have to pay the winner. However, the record is usually provided* free of charge *in criminal cases. Ask your lawyer for the rules of your particular jurisdiction.*

- The lawyers file briefs (written arguments) with the court.
- After all of the briefs have been filed, a hearing is held where the lawyers give oral arguments and answer questions hurled at them by the justices (Appellate judges).
- Ultimately a written decision is issued by the court which sets forth their reasons for affirming or reversing the case.

Most cases end here. A very few move on up the Appeals Court ladder, all the way to the U.S. Supreme Court.

Your lawyer's responsibilities "on Appeal" include:

- properly preparing and filing the Notice of Appeal.
- properly identifying documents to be included in the record.
- making sure the record has been properly prepared and forwarded to the Court of Appeal.
- thoroughly reviewing the record to find errors.
- researching the law.
- preparing a brief and filing it on time.

HINT: *Failure to meet time deadlines can result in having an Appeal dismissed or heard without input from the lawyer who missed the deadline.*

- reviewing the opposition's brief for errors in fact or law.
- appearing at the hearing prepared to answer any questions that might be asked by the justices.
- explaining the court's decision to you in a way you can understand.
- if you lost, recommending whether to try again or give up.

HINT: *Appeals, especially in civil cases, involve a great deal of time and money. It hardly pays to spend $8,000 appealing a Judgment against you of $10,000.*

- collecting costs on Appeal if awarded against the other side.

POTPOURRI

While trial lawyers get all the glory, lawyers who sit in offices *preventing* lawsuits from happening provide just as, if not more, valuable a service. Here's some of what they do.

Negotiating agreements

Let's say you want to buy a house or small business, and you decide to "save money" and handle the matter yourself. One year later, you discover you've been had. You sue, and $8,000 (and much heartache) later, you win the case. Well, all that trouble might have been avoided if you had paid a lawyer to negotiate and prepare the agreement for you. Remember, an ounce of prevention is *always* worth a pound of cure. Let a lawyer negotiate.

Preparing legal documents

Many legal documents, such as a Trust or Deed, rise or fall on the choice of words used in the document itself. In such cases, lawyers are worth their weight in gold (or ink, whatever the case may be).

Giving advice

Sometimes you just need a trained ear to listen to you and let you know whether you are on the right track or about to fall off a cliff. Part of a lawyer's job is to act as a sounding board.

Acting as a source of referrals

Lawyers frequently come into contact with other professionals and experts in various fields. This sometimes makes them an excellent source of referrals. Thus, if you need a good doctor to handle your sprained back, a lawyer who works in the field of personal injury may guide you to the best—and steer you away from the worst. Lawyers are also an excellent source of referrals to other lawyers.

Giving personal recommendations

If you are close to a lawyer—be it a business or personal relationship—and need a personal recommendation, consider asking the lawyer to make it for you. His or her word may often carry a lot of weight.

WARNING!

This concludes our discussion of what lawyers do. Please remember, it is only intended to give you an *overview* of your lawyer's world. It is definitely *not* a complete discussion of the subject, nor is it intended to tell you exactly what will happen in your particular case—*that only your lawyer can do.* So please, do yourself a favor—*ask!*

8

KEEPING TRACK
USING THE DUPLICATE FILE SYSTEM

CLIENTUS PARANOIDUS

If there is one thing that drives clients absolutely crazy, it is being kept in the dark about what is going on with their own case. This leads to a form of hysteria which I have termed *"clientus paranoidus"*—a condition in which the client becomes convinced that his or her lawyer is on the take or, worse, is really Benedict Arnold in disguise.

Together, you and your lawyer can stamp out this insidious form of disease. All it requires is some communication, mutual understanding and *an organized approach to your case.*

It's easy for your lawyer to be organized. He or she has a secretary (God bless them one and all)—but you probably don't—so try this simple and painless step by step approach.

FIRST, BUY THE FOLLOWING:

1. One 3–Ring Notebook
2. One 3–Hole Punch
3. One Packet of Divider Tabs
4. One Package of Notebook Paper

SECOND, DIVIDE THE NOTEBOOK INTO THE FOLLOWING SECTIONS, LABELING THE DIVIDER TABS ACCORDINGLY.

1. RETAINER AGREEMENT
2. MONTHLY BILLS
3. NOTES
4. LETTERS
5. PLEADINGS
6. DOCUMENTS
7. CALENDAR

NOW YOU ARE READY TO GO!

The Retainer Agreement

With your three–hole punch, punch holes in your Retainer Agreement. File it in Section One of your notebook, along with the notes you took when you discussed the Agreement with your lawyer. In this way, if a question ever comes up about your rights and duties under the Retainer Agreement, you'll know just where to look.

Here's an example of what I mean. Suppose you receive a note from your lawyer which states:

> Payment on your costs account is past due. Please remit $750 forthwith as repayment of all costs advanced to date. (If payment has already been made, please disregard this notice.)

"How can payment have already been made?!" you shout, *"I didn't know I owed the money!"*

But then you calm down. After all, being an intelligent client (and having read this book), you realize that the Retainer Agreement controls the terms of your financial understanding with your lawyer. You take your notebook off of the pedestal on which you keep it, and immediately turn to Section One—where you find your copy of the Retainer Agreement. Therein (lawyerese for "in the document"), you find the following language in the section on costs:

> Client is responsible for payment of all costs advanced by the lawyer within 30 days of demand. Lawyer shall not incur costs in excess of $250 per item without permission of client in advance. Lawyer will provide client with copies of all receipts for costs incurred, upon request.

You look up your notes about what you and your lawyer discussed regarding costs, and you find that you wrote down the following:

> *Lawyer will pay costs and ask me to pay him back to save time.*

He doesn't expect the costs to get expensive unless he has to take depositions.

Agreed that I have to give him permission before he can spend a single cost of more than $250 on one cost item.

"Aha!," you say to yourself. "Something smells rotten in Denmark!"

And you may take note of the following:

- Under the Retainer Agreement you have thirty days in which to repay costs. Thus, the request for "forthwith" payment is improper.
- Under the Retainer Agreement, you are entitled to be consulted *before* an individual cost that exceeds $250 can be incurred. You were never asked to approve such a cost, and you will want to find out if such a cost was incurred without permission, and if so, why.
- You are entitled to review the cost receipts. You will want to ask for them.
- Your notes tell you that your lawyer told you that he did not expect the costs to get expensive until depositions had been taken—none, to your knowledge have been taken. You will want to ask why the costs advanced are so high.

You could then telephone your lawyer and, using your notes, politely discuss the difficulties you had with his or her request.

HINT: *If a lawyer makes a mistake in his or her financial dealings with you, he or she will usually be more than happy to correct it. If your lawyer won't, it's probably a good sign that you selected the wrong lawyer.*

Monthly Bills

No, receiving a detailed monthly billing statement is *not* a form of Chinese Water Torture. It's a method of protection, and a valuable source of information about your case. That is why you will want to review each monthly bill as you receive it and then file it promptly in your notebook.

Here are some of the ways the system I propose will serve you.

As protection

Lawyers rarely intentionally cheat in their billing, but mistakes do happen. A common mistake is for a charge which is made "on the cusp" between two billing periods, to be listed at the end of one month's statement and at the beginning of another. By comparing the monthly bills, you can correct such an error, should it occur.

Monthly bills can also be a tool to help prevent your lawyer from inadvertently (or purposefully) charging more time on your account than was actually spent.

Every time you interact with your lawyer, you should take notes about what happened, or what was discussed—which you will file in your notebook under "Notes" (clever title, eh?). One of the items you will be *sure* to write down is the *time* you and your lawyer spent on your case—be it at a court appearance or a telephone call. For example an entry in your notes could begin like this:

March 10—Office conference with lawyer—30 minutes

When your bill arrived, you would compare time charged by your lawyer with the time you wrote in your notes. If they don't agree, find out why.

Of course, much of the time, you will not be present when your lawyer works on your case. But remember, you have instructed your lawyer to send you copies of all of the paperwork generated in your case. So, when you receive your monthly bill, and you find you have been charged for an item such as "Letter to Opposing Counsel" or "Reviewed Letter From Opposing Counsel" or "Preparation of Complaint"—you will check your records to make sure you received a copy of the document in question. You will also look at the document to see if the charge made seems reasonable. (If you receive a copy of a two-paragraph letter and are charged $100 on your bill, that is *probably not* reasonable—but a charge of $30 may be. If in doubt, *ask*.)

As information
If you keep all of your monthly billing in chronological order, they will serve as a history of what your lawyer did for you during your case. Thus, if you have a question whether something your lawyer promised to do was actually done, just check your bills. (After all, if it was done, it was billed!)

As evidence
If you ever have a dispute with your lawyer, whether it involves alleged malpractice (negligent representation), a fee dispute or a simple case of lawyer laziness (not getting the work done), your bills will serve as important evidence about what happened during your case (in conjunction with the rest of your duplicate file).

For taxes
On the positive side, some services you pay your lawyer for *may* be tax deductible (ask your lawyer or accountant for specifics). If they are, and you claim them, the I.R.S.

may force you to prove it! The bills you receive and keep should more than satisfy even the most hardened and cynical I.R.S. agent.

Notes

I know this sounds like I'm a teacher asking you to do homework, but *please make a habit of taking notes* whenever you talk to your lawyer. Believe me, it's well worth your time.

The notes do not have to be in any special form (I won't even be checking for spelling), but they should contain the following information:

- The *date* of the conference, court appearance or phone call.
- The *length of time* involved (to check against the monthly bill).
- A *summary* of what was discussed.

Here are a few examples of what I mean:

JUNE 8—TELEPHONE CALL WITH LAWYER
TIME—2 MINUTES

I asked him whether we had received an answer to our offer of settlement. He said no, that he would call Creep Face's lawyer and call me back. I told him that I don't appreciate having to wait—that I wanted to go to trial. He asked me to be patient.

JUNE 9—TELEPHONE CALL FROM LAWYER
TIME—10 MINUTES

Creep Face wants to settle, but will only offer me $15,000. I asked my lawyer what he thought. He said that after I paid fees and costs, I'd have $11,000 in my pocket. And that at trial he thought I could win $25,000.

I asked how much of the $25,000 would end up in my pocket. He said about $18,000. He figured a trial would cost about $4,000 in fees.

I asked what he thought my chances were at trial. He said about 70%. I asked if I could lose. He said yes, if the jury didn't believe my version of the story.

I told him I'd call him after I thought it over.

The client here has a decision to make. Having the notes to look at can help him or her decide.

Also, he or she can "look back in time" and see what the lawyer said before, to see if there has now been a big change in the lawyer's position. For example, if the lawyer once said the case "is worth $100,000," the client would want to find out what exactly changed the lawyer's opinion about the case.

JUNE 9—CALLED DAD

I asked Dad what he thought. He said $11,000 was a lot of money. He'd take it and run.

> **HINT:** *Sometimes when making a decision, we talk to those close to us for advice. It never hurts to write it down.*

JUNE 9—CALLED TED
Ted said Creep Face had really cheated and lied to me. That I shouldn't let him get away with it. I pointed out that I need to buy a new car, and that the $11,000 could do that. He said $18,000 would buy a better car.

JUNE 9—CALLED LAWYER
TIME—5 MINUTES
I told him I will take it, but that I want as much money as he can get. He said he'd try to counter offer at $20,000. I said okay.

JUNE 10—CALL FROM LAWYER
TIME—4 MINUTES
Case settled at $18,000! Hawaii here I come! Lawyer said the money will arrive by July 1st.

> **HINT:** *The date of July 1 is important, and should be noted in his or her calendar.*

Be sure you deposit your notes in chronological order as you go along. In that way you can always look back and see whether the case is proceeding according to plan.

Recap

I cannot overstate how important it is to keep notes about your case. Not only will a review of your notes be able to answer a question you might have (thereby saving money because you won't have to ask your lawyer), but it will help you in making sure that promises are kept. It will also assist you in recalling events, sometimes years later, should you have a dispute with your lawyer.

Letters

In the fairy tale *Hansel and Gretel,* two children are forced to enter a deep dark forest where they fear they will be lost. But, being bright and enterprising children, they decide to leave a bread crumb trail so that they can find their way out again. Like the heroes of the story, you too should leave a trail—a paper trail—in the wake of your business dealings (be it with your lawyer, plumber or friendly banker), from which you can retrace your steps, should the need arise.

You create a paper trail by keeping a written record of the oral requests, promises and agreements that are part of your business relationship—most particularly your attorney-client relationship—by writing or requesting what is known as "the confirming letter."

Suppose you told your lawyer on the phone that an important witness would be leaving in six weeks on a one-year-around-the-world trip. Your lawyer's response was, "Then we'd better take her deposition before she leaves." You would write a letter to your lawyer, "confirming" the contents of the conversation, which might read something like this:

> Ms. My Only Hope
> Attorney At Law
> 1111 Expect a Miracle Place
> Justice, Missouri
> March 6, 19____

Dear Ms. Hope,

Just a note to confirm the contents of our phone conversation of yesterday in which I informed you that my friend, Wants To Talk, is leaving in six weeks for a one year trip around the world (I should be so lucky). You told me that we should take her deposition before she leaves. I agree. Please let me know when the deposition will be taking place so we can meet to discuss the matter.

> Sincerely,
>
> *Outta Luck*

HINT: *Hansel and Gretel made one mistake—they used bread crumbs to make their trail, which the birds quickly ate. If you don't make a copy of your letter, it too, could "disappear," should trouble arise—thus, be sure to make use of the "magic" of twentieth-century technology. Have the letter photocopied, and file it in your notebook under "Letters."*

HINT: *Don't worry about offending your lawyer by writing a confirming letter. If you make a promise to your lawyer, or your lawyer requests important action from you, believe me, you too will receive a confirming letter—known in "secret lawyer counsels" as "CYA" letters (Cover Your A . . .). File these in your notebook, too.*

HINT: *Lawyers also send CYA letters to other lawyers all of the time during the course of a case. Copies should be sent to you, which you should file. By the time your case is over, your section labeled "Letters" should contain a complete history of the case.*

Pleadings

I'm sure you've all heard that "an army moves on its stomach." Well, "lawsuits move on their pleadings" (documents filed with the court). So, if you want to know where your lawsuit is—or is not—on the "trail to trial," be sure you receive copies of all pleadings and other court documents, and file them in your notebook. If you do, you will have a copy of what is in the court's file, which is the official history of the case. Keeping a record of the pleadings can also prove very helpful to you as the case progresses.

Here is a hypothetical situation to illustrate what I mean.

Suppose your lawyer advised you to "sue the heck" out of your former employer who fired you because he didn't like the gap between your front teeth. Your lawyer thinks of twelve "Causes of Action" (different legal reasons why you are entitled to receive money) to include in the Complaint. You have, of course, taken notes on the meeting, asked questions and, if you really read this chapter, have sent (or asked for) a confirming letter on the subject.

Later, you sign the Complaint and take a copy home for your files. Since there's nothing on TV that night, you decide to review the Complaint, and lo and behold, you find it only has *eleven* Causes of Action, a fact you missed at the lawyer's office (because you fell in love with his secretary, or his office furniture or whatever). You would then call your lawyer and find out why the Twelfth Cause of Action is missing.

HINT: *Don't ever think lawyers don't make mistakes—they do. So, think of your review of your lawyer's work as a back-up safety system. You're not telling him or her how to do his or her job, you're just making sure your lawyer does the job you were told would be done.*

Or, suppose you were told by your lawyer that the Complaint (which now contains all twelve Causes of Action) was served on your former employer, Orthodontic Braces Manufacturing Inc., on May 1st, and that your lawyer should receive a copy of the Answer from them by June 2nd. If you have not received your copy of their Answer from your lawyer by June 5th, you would call your lawyer to find out why.

Let's assume that a copy of the Answer does arrive. You look it over and see that your former employer alleges you were fired because of "insubordination," specifically regarding an incident where you are alleged to have told the founder of Orthodontic Braces Manufacturing Inc. that "braces are a form of torture," and that you hoped God would punish him after death by forcing him to "wear braces for eternity." You remember the incident, what was *really* said and who witnessed it. So, you contact your lawyer and give him the information he needs to take action to rebut these slanderous lies.

Your lawyer tells you the action that will be taken, which includes the taking of a deposition. You receive from your lawyer (pursuant to your request for copies of all pleadings) a document called a "Notice of Deposition" which tells you that the deposition of Johnny Bigears, who heard the whole thing, will be taken on July 6th. You then make arrangements to be there so you can hear first hand what Bigears has to say.

You also receive a copy of a Notice of Deposition filed by the other side, which states that the deposition of Charlie Fibber will be taken on July 8th. Your lawyer includes with your copy of the notice a note which says, "Who's that?" It's the nephew of your former boss who has hated you since you beat him for the post of "Senior Class President" in high school. You write your lawyer a three-page letter giving him examples of what a liar Charlie is—examples your lawyer uses to discredit him for the "fibber" he is—at the deposition.

And so it goes. Your receipt of every court document adds to the paper trail of the case and to your knowledge of "who is doing what to whom." You may not understand everything you receive, but that problem is simple to overcome—ask questions.

Documents

If you sometimes get the sinking feeling that the business of America is . . . paperwork, then imagine how your poor lawyer must feel. He or she usually has to review reams of it during the preparation of a case. If you learn that some of the documents (letters, bank records, inventory lists, whatever) have been found—which are key—ask for a copy.

Having copies of important documents can be very helpful to both your lawyer and you, because when the time comes to separate the "wheat" of the paperwork from the "chaff," you'll already have most of the "wheat" filed in your notebook. Plus, when you and your lawyer review the documents you wish to present in court, your file can serve as a back-up system, which catches a document that may be missing in your lawyer's file. (Yes, things do fall between the cracks in lawyers' offices. If you knew how often, you wouldn't think twice about asking for copies of all important documents.)

Another good reason for you to receive copies of key documents is this—you will be able to review them and perhaps catch things your lawyer might miss. Remember, your lawyer handles many clients' cases at once (or goes out of business), and so he or she cannot hope to spend as much time as you can reviewing documents. More important, you may very well have more insight into what a document means than your lawyer does— especially if the document contains technical language, or "terms of art" used in a particular field.

HINT: *Lawyers, especially civil trial lawyers, are by necessity "students." One case may concern real estate, the next, the faulty design of a product, and so on. If your case involves specialized terms or information, don't hesitate to educate your lawyer about what they mean. After all, knowledge truly is power.*

Some of what you receive from your lawyer may be a "pleading," which for our purposes I define as "that which is filed with a court and is thus part of the court's record"—or a "document" which I define as "a document or record which is *not* 'filed' with the court." Don't worry if you don't know which is which. All that's really important is that you receive copies of all important papers and file them in such a way that you can find them when the need arises.

Calendar

If you ever have had a chance to observe lawyers at close range, you will note that their lives are controlled by their calendars. Lawyers are lost without their calendars, for within them, lawyers (or their secretaries) write down all of what they will be doing in the days, weeks and months to follow. As lawyers do for their practice, you should do for your case. Thus, your notebook should contain a calendar, so you can write down what will be happening and when. (You can even use a wall calendar if you want—I won't be offended.)

Thus, if your lawyer tells you something will occur at a specific time, *write the date in your calendar*. If you have to be in court, *write the date in your calendar*. If you have to give your lawyer some information—well, you get the point.

Keeping a calendar has many benefits, for example:

- You will be able to keep your "life" from conflicting with your "case." For instance, if you are planning a trip to Europe, you can look on your calendar to make sure you don't find yourself at the Leaning Tower of Pisa, instead of on the witness stand.
- You will be able to make sure your lawyer performs as promised.
- You will be able to make sure you don't forget deadlines of your own. Remember, if your lawyer asks you to do something within a specified time, it's usually because he or she is working against a time deadline. Thus, your tardiness can make your lawyer tardy, which never helps you and which can hurt you—and hurt you badly!
- You will have a complete record of what occurred (or didn't) should that ever become an issue.

HELPFUL HINTS REGARDING YOU AND YOUR NOTEBOOK

Keeping your own file is not as hard as it may seem, IF:

- You file things promptly as received. In other words, don't do as I do in my personal life, which is to throw things in a box to be sorted out later. Remember, "later," like "tomorrow," often never comes.
- You keep your records in chronological order.
- You index the most important documents.

Here is how to do it:

1. Buy small tabs.
2. Attach them to each document you wish to be able to find instantly.
3. Assign the document a number or a letter.
4. Write the number or letter on the tab.
5. Keep an index of what document is represented by which number, and file it at the front of your notebook.

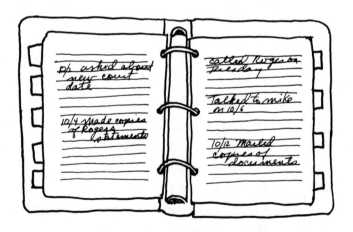

It might look like the following if you were involved in a civil case surrounding the end of a partnership:

INDEX

NUMBER   DOCUMENT

1.   Complaint
2.   Answer
3.   Bank records of partner (YEAR)
4.   Bank records of partner (FOLLOWING YEAR)
5.   Bank records of business (YEAR)
6.   Bank records of business (FOLLOWING YEAR)
7.   Copy of letter from accountant (DATE)
8.   My answers to interrogatories
9.   My notes with lawyer about settlement

HINT: *In very large cases, the paperwork generated can fill filing cabinets. If you have the misfortune to be a part of such a mess, you will still want to keep your own file—but you may want to edit down what you put into it—to include only the most important items.*

A Note About Depositions:

The length of depositions can range from about fifty pages to several volumes of three hundred and fifty or so pages each. So it may not be practical to keep copies of them all. However, you should read them all, and make notes of what was said—which you can file in your notebook.

Now that you have an organized approach, let's take a closer look at how you can put it to effective use!

9

RIDING HERD
MAKING SURE THE JOB GETS DONE

I'm a big fan of horror movies, but I saw one the other night that was almost too much for me to stomach. It was called:

(And the ad poster screamed:)

"HE PROMISED HER EVERYTHING. . . . AND THEN WENT GOLFING!"

The plot was about a young co-ed who hired a lawyer to stop a bank from foreclosing on her grandfather's farm. Unfortunately for the old man, the lawyer didn't file the papers on time, and "Umpa," as he was affectionately known, was tossed into the street. This made the co-ed so upset that she turned into a zombie who attacked a local Bar Association convention. (I didn't stay for the end of the movie, because at that point the audience started cheering so loudly that I couldn't hear the dialogue. But it was when they started checking people's wallets for Bar membership cards that I knew it was time to leave. . . .)

Unfortunately, "The Lawyer From Hell" isn't a total fantasy. Sometimes, lawyers *do* make promises which they *do not keep*. Part of your job as a client is to keep this from happening to you. . . .

STAYING INVOLVED

The best way to keep lawyers on their toes is to let them know you are looking over their shoulders—*not* in the sense of telling them what to do—that would be stupid— but by letting your lawyer know, by word and deed, that you expect him or her to follow through with the action the two of you have agreed should be taken.

This is where much of what we have already discussed comes together. So, let's follow a client who is going through a divorce, as she works with her lawyer during the case.

June 1st:
Our heroine, Janice Jilted, has just retained Letme Atim to represent her against her husband, Ralph. She has paid Letme a $750 retainer fee, and she is being charged $125 per hour, which will be billed against the retainer. She has her copy of the Retainer Agreement, and understands the document completely. She continues to take notes as she and Letme conclude their conference . . .

JANICE: *"So, what are you going to do first?"*

LETME: *"File a Petition for Divorce, and file an O.S.C. to ask for temporary alimony.*

Janice writes down this information. But she doesn't know what an O.S.C. means.

JANICE: *"What's an O.S.C.?"*

LETME: *"It means Order to Show Cause. It's a court hearing where we can get some temporary orders for alimony, pending the divorce.*

Janice looks at her notes from the earlier part of the conversation.

JANICE: *"You said you thought I would be able to get $500 a month in alimony. Is that what I'll get at this hearing?"*

LETME: *"Well, I'm asking for $600, but it depends on Ralph's wages; there's no guarantee. I'll subpoena his records."*

JANICE: *"Fine. When will you file the papers?"*

LETME: *"Monday the 6th."*

JANICE: *"Good. Would you send copies to me, please?"*

LETME: *"Sure."*

JANICE: *"Will you also please have your secretary call me with the date and time of the hearing so I can put it in my calendar?"*

LETME: *"Right."*

JANICE: *"Thank you. I look forward to working with you. My uncle recommended you very highly."*

LETME: *"Please give him my regards when you see him. Good-bye."*

Janice, being a well informed client, goes home and sets up her Client Duplicate File Notebook. She:

- deposits her Retainer Agreement and her notes about that document in their proper place.
- deposits her notes in the "Notes" section.
- marks the following on her calendar:

June 8—Should know court date
June 9—Should have copies of papers

Janice goes about her business. June 8th comes and goes. On June 9th, Janice calls her lawyer. She takes notes as she speaks.

June 9th:

JANICE: *"Ms. Atim, this is Janice Jilted."*

LETME: *"Oh yes, how are you?"*

JANICE: *"Very well, thank you. I'm calling because I haven't received word about my O.S.C."*

LETME: *"Yes, well, I haven't received the paperwork back from the court yet."*

JANICE: *"How long does that usually take?"*

LETME: *"Two days or so."*

JANICE: *"When were the papers filed?"*

LETME: *"Yesterday."*

JANICE: *"Oh? I thought you said you'd file them by the 6th?"*

LETME: *"Yes, I'm sorry about that. I had an emergency come up, a wife beating case, and I fell a little behind."*

JANICE: *"Oh, I understand. I hope things worked out okay. Would you call me when the papers arrive? I'll sleep better knowing things are on track."*

LETME: *"No problem. Sorry about the delay."*

Janice hangs up, puts her notes of the conversation—including the time—"two minutes"—into her notebook.

> **HINT:** *This conversation told the lawyer a great deal about her client:*
> - *That she remembered what she told her.*
> - *That she was going to hold her to her word.*
> - *That she wanted to be kept informed.*
> - *That she realized that the unforeseen can arise, and that she understood that sometimes the lawyer's priorities have to be with other clients.*

June 10th:

Janice receives a message on her answering machine, that:

- the court date is set for June 25th at 9:00 AM
- Letme wants to meet with her a day or two beforehand, to prepare.

Janice puts a check mark (✓) in her calendar by the June 8th entry, with "should know court date"—indicating to her that her lawyer's promise had been kept.

She then calls her lawyer and sets an appointment for June 24th at 4:30 PM, which she writes in her calendar, along with the court date.

Two days later, Janice receives her copies of the "Petition" and the O.S.C. She reviews the petition—all is as planned—but when she reviews the O.S.C., she finds a mistake! Instead of asking for $600 per month, the request is for $60!

Janice immediately calls Letme and is informed that she will be out of town until June 15th. Janice explains the problem to the secretary (Janice doesn't yell or scream, but tells the secretary she is very concerned). The secretary promises to have Letme call Janice as soon as Letme can be reached.

Two hours later, Letme calls. Here is a partial copy of the notes Janice took about the conversation:

June 12th:

June 12th—Conversation with Letme Atim

- *Letme was upset—said it was a typo error.*
- *She said the Hearing would have to be postponed, unless Ralph's lawyer would okay an amendment to the papers.*
- *She's had cases with Ralph's lawyer before, so there should be no problem.*
- *She'll call me back right away.*

Twenty minutes later, Letme informs Janice that Ralph's lawyer okayed the amendment.

Ralph's lawyer gave Letme what is known as a "professional courtesy." This is good for Ralph, because there was little to be gained fighting the amendment (except incurring additional attorney's fees); good for Ralph's lawyer (on the theory that "what goes around comes around"); and good for Letme and Janice.

If your lawyer appears to be friendly with his or her counterpart, don't worry. Their friendship will not prevent your lawyer from doing his or her best for you. Besides, things usually "go better" when the lawyers get along.

Janice is pleased that everything turned out well, but is unhappy that the mistake occurred. She decides in the interest of maintaining a good relationship with her lawyer, not to make an issue of it. But, *she also puts a reminder to herself in the "Bills" section of her notebook to make sure she is not charged for the time it took to correct her lawyer's error.*

June 19th:

Janice receives copies of Ralph's pleadings in response to her petition and O.S.C. She compares the documents and notes the following:

June 19th—Ralph says car is worth $8,000. We only paid $7,000 for it 2 years ago.

Ralph didn't show on his financial statement that he works overtime regularly.

Ralph only willing to pay $150 a month!!

She deposits the pleadings from Ralph in her notebook and calls her lawyer.

JANICE: *"Letme, I just received Ralph's papers, and boy is he full of . . ."*

LETME: *"Alright, calm down. I told you this would probably happen."*

JANICE: *"Can he get away with $150?"*

LETME: *"I seriously doubt it."*

JANICE: *"Did I tell you he usually works overtime?"*

LETME: *"Yes."*

JANICE: *"You did subpoena his records like you said you would, didn't you?"*

LETME: *"Yes. The records will be available at the hearing. Now calm down and I'll see you on the 24th."*

JANICE: *"Okay. I'm sorry I bothered you."*

LETME: *"No bother, that's what I'm here for."*

Janice hangs up and notes the phone conversation took three minutes. She writes it down in her notes and files them. She also notes that Letme had *not* sent her a copy of the subpoena.

HINT: *Handholding is part of your lawyer's job. Your lawyer is entitled to charge for the call in hourly rate cases, even if nothing of "substance" occurred.*

June 24th:
Janice and Letme meet to confer about the case, and she tells her in detail everything that will happen. Janice asks questions about what she doesn't understand. She also

brings the notes about Ralph's pleadings, and talks about them with Letme. Letme comments:

LETME: *"I'll cross-examine Ralph about his overtime tomorrow when I have him on the witness stand. I'll deal with the value of the car at Ralph's deposition."*

Janice, of course, takes notes—including the fact that the conference lasted 45 minutes.

June 25th:

The big day arrives. In court, the judge orders Ralph to pay Janice $475 per month in alimony. The judge also orders the parties to be ready for trial on October 5th. Janice wants to be sure that she understands what is going to happen, so she asks her lawyer to tell her specifically what is planned between then and trial. Letme tells Janice that she will:

- obtain the court order from the clerk
- take Ralph's deposition
- take the accountant's deposition
- review Ralph's bank accounts
- hire a business appraiser

Janice writes it all down. She also requests a copy of the court order. She then asks Letme what she will do first. Letme tells Janice she will take Ralph's deposition. Let's listen in on part of their conversation:

JANICE: *"When will you know the date of Ralph's deposition?"*

LETME: *"In a week or so, definitely by July 10th."*

JANICE: *"What do you expect it to cost?"*

LETME: *"$350, unless it goes on longer than I anticipate. But you realize that I can't promise to limit the time I spend. It all depends on how Ralph answers."*

JANICE: *"Oh, I understand. I just want to know what's ahead—that's very important to me."*

Janice writes in her calendar for July 10th:

- *Ralph's deposition set? (   )*
- *Court order received? (   )*

July 3rd:

Janice receives her first bill. She writes a check mark (✓) beside each charge on the bill she agrees is reasonable. She finds, thanks to her earlier reminder to herself, that she *was* charged by Letme for thirty minutes worth of work for the time it took to correct the error regarding the alimony request! Janice immediately calls Letme:

LETME: *"What can I do for you, Janice?"*

JANICE: *"I just discovered a mistake on my bill."*

LETME: *"Really? What?"*

JANICE: *"You charged me 30 minutes for the time it took to correct the mistake on the O.S.C."*

LETME: *"I'm very sorry. I'll instruct the bookkeeper to correct your bill. The correction will appear on your next statement."*

JANICE: *"Thank you. I don't think I should be charged for this call either."*

LETME: *"You won't. Again, I'm sorry for the trouble."*

JANICE: *"Thank you."*

Janice decides that she should write a confirming letter, just in case. (The form of the letter is not what's important. The fact that it's in writing, and you keep a copy, *is*.)

> **HINT:** *This letter is businesslike in tone, and will serve to remind Letme of her responsibilities. Don't be afraid to write, because lawyers sometimes do forget.*

July 3rd 19____
Ms. Letme Atim
Atim, Scarem & Smith
1111 Trustme Ave.
Central Falls, R.I. (zip code)

Dear Letme,

Thank you for agreeing to remove the June 12th thirty-minute charge, which was incurred to correct the error in the O.S.C. papers. Your prompt attention to my concerns is appreciated.

I also wish to confirm that I will not be charged for today's phone call in which I pointed out the error.

Has the deposition been set?

Sincerely,

Janice Jilted

Janice Jilted

July 8th:

Janice received her copy of the court order and marked a (✔) by the reminder to herself she had written in her calendar.

July 10th:

Janice notes that she should have heard about Ralph's deposition, but hasn't. She calls her lawyer.

  LETME: *"Hi, Janice."*

  JANICE: *"Any news about Ralph's deposition?"*

  LETME: *"Shoot! I've been in trial, and I didn't get it done! I'll be back to you tomorrow with a date. I promise."*

  JANICE: *"Please do."*

They hang up. Letme calls her secretary on the intercom:

"Paul, please call Ralph Jilted's lawyer and see if August 1st is okay for Ralph's deposition. If so, call Janice Jilted and let her know, okay? Also, tell her the time has come for her to send me Ralph's cancelled checks for the last two years."

HINT: *Janice may sound pushy to you, but believe me, most lawyers will take immediate action on a client's case, if they are made to realize that they have not fully performed as promised.*

July 11th:
The message about the deposition date and the request for the checks is passed on to Janice, who puts both in

Dear Letme,
As you requested
I have enclosed all
of Ralph's cancelled
checks...

her calendar. She then gathers the checks together to bring to Letme. Before doing so, however, *she writes a cover letter*.

When you are giving your lawyer a document or any other physical item (or piece of evidence), always get a receipt, have photocopies made or write a letter identifying the items delivered. In this way, a "chain of possession" can be established so that in the event something ever gets lost, you will know who is supposed to have it. (Lawyers use cover letters to protect their backsides—you should too!)

> July 11th 19____
> Ms. Letme Atim
> Atim, Scarem & Smith
> 1111 Trustme Ave.
> Central Falls, R.I.

Dear Letme,

As you requested, I have enclosed all of Ralph's cancelled checks for the last two years. Please take good care of them; they are the only records I have about our financial affairs. In fact, would you photocopy them just in case?

> Thanks,
>
> *Janice*

Janice keeps a copy of the cover letter and files it in her notebook under "Letters."

HINT: *Make it a habit to write COVER LETTERS in ALL of your business affairs. They are an important part of any "paper trail."*

July 18th
Janice makes an urgent call to her lawyer:

JANICE: *"I just remembered! Ralph and I once owned a second dry cleaners, but we sold it two years ago."*

LETME: *"What happened to the money?"*

JANICE: *"I don't know for sure. Ralph told me he lost it in a stock investment, but he's lied to me before."*

LETME: *"How much was involved?"*

JANICE: *"$15,000!"*

LETME: *"Janice, this is very important, try to remember everything you can about the transaction, and let me know all of the details, okay?"*

Janice hangs up and searches her mind about the details surrounding the sale of the other business. She takes her time, and writes down in her notes all of the details she can remember. As soon as she feels she has recalled all that she can, she sits down and writes a letter, using her notes to make sure she doesn't leave anything out.

HINT: *I believe it is always a good idea to set forth in writing all important information you give your lawyer. Not only does it establish that your lawyer was given the information if something goes wrong, but more important, it can help to* prevent *a problem by highlighting the information in your lawyer's mind.*

Thus, this type of confirming letter can serve as a "failsafe." After all, it's always better to be safe than sorry.

Recap
So, what has Janice accomplished by taking the extra effort to "ride herd?" Well, for one thing, her use of the Client Duplicate File Notebook and the specific and timely nature of her questions kept her lawyer on her toes and on the case. It also saved Janice some money.

But most important, it kept Janice at the *cause* rather than the *effect* of her case. By that I mean this—Janice always knew what was going on, therefore she wasn't left with that horrible helpless feeling of "dangling slowly in the wind." So, while her life certainly wasn't great (after all, divorces are never fun), the stress in her life wasn't worsened by having to fight a two-front war—against her husband and her own fears.

Keeping on top of things is no guarantee that nothing will go wrong, but it does *reduce the chances.*

HAPPY ENDING! Janice and Ralph were so fed up with lawyers, they ended up going to a marriage counselor and getting back together again. They now live happily in Rhode Island, where she handles their invest-ments and their checkbook.

JUDGING YOUR LAWYER'S WORK

The concept of "riding herd" isn't just limited to making sure the job gets done—it also has to do with making sure the job *gets done right*. Don't worry, I'm not asking you to go to law school—I wouldn't wish that torture on anyone—but I am asking you to pay close attention, and to judge the quality of your lawyer's work.

Is Your Lawyer Prepared?

Your lawyer's work on your case can be compared to a baseball player's performance on the field. The more work and preparation that he or she puts in before a game, the better chance of hitting a home run.

Now, obviously, you can't transform yourself into the proverbial "fly on the wall" and watch your lawyer's every move—but you can judge whether your lawyer is adequately prepared. One way is to discuss the case with him or her *before* a court appointment or other event.

Another way to assure yourself that your lawyer is prepared is to watch him or her in action—that means you must take the time to be with your lawyer as often as you can. When he or she is in court on your case, or at a deposition or other important proceeding, and you get the feeling that your lawyer had trouble keeping his or her head above water—it may be time for a serious talk.

HINT: *Lawyers conduct their business during normal working hours, thus you may have to take time off of work to be present in court or at a deposition. This is not always practical, so, if you do not attend, make sure you contact your lawyer after the event and get all the details. If it appears something was missed, ask if it was—then, find out why. Also, if a transcript is prepared of a proceeding you missed (or even attended) be sure to read it—it will tell you a lot about your lawyer's performance.*

Does Your Lawyer Get Work Done On Time?

While "better late than never" is usually true, "better on time than late" is always true. Thus, if you find that your lawyer is consistently late in getting his or her work done, or always has to ask for more time to prepare, you'd better take a good hard look at the quality of the work produced—even if it means taking it to another lawyer to review.

HINT: *If a lawyer is late, he or she will try to compensate by working faster than usual. Thus, when you review the work, make sure you check and double-check your list of "issues" to make sure nothing was missed.*

If you find that your lawyer's work is consistently late:

- make follow-up calls a day or two before the "due date." It might go something like this:

CLIENT: *"Hi, Mr. Slowpoke, this is Uptight."*

LAWYER: *"Oh, yeah, how are ya?"*

CLIENT: *"Fine. I was just calling to discuss the motion you are filing. Is it prepared yet? I'd like to read it."*

LAWYER: *"No, I'm working on it right now." (He says as he eats his sandwich.)*

CLIENT: *"Can I come in tomorrow afternoon, then?"*

LAWYER: *"Oh yeah, sure thing."*

CLIENT: *"Great, see you then. Bye."*

They hang up. Slowpoke calls his secretary.

LAWYER: *"Judy, bring me Uptight's file, will ya? I better get to work on it."*

Like I've said, if a lawyer knows you're watching, chances are he or she will do his or her best.

• write a letter of complaint to your lawyer:

> December 6, 19____
> Mr. Bob Slowpoke
> Slowpoke & Molasses
> Attorneys at Law
> 452 Glacier Lane
> Kickim, Conn.

Dear Mr. Slowpoke,

A problem exists that I feel I must discuss with you. Your work never seems to get done when you say it will. For example, I told you that my friend, Susan Reliable, who was in the car when I was rear ended, was moving to Mt. Kilimanjaro in November. You told me you would take her deposition in October. You didn't, and now she's on safari. This is just one example of your tardy performance. In the future, I expect you to show me the respect I deserve, by doing work on my case in a timely fashion.

Thank you,

John Uptight

HINT: *If your lawyer receives such a letter, and he or she cares about your business, believe me, your case will be permanently "on the front burner." If your lawyer's reaction to a bona fide letter of complaint is to tell you to "take this file and stuff it," well, you're probably better off with another lawyer anyway.*

HINT: *Don't try to "bully" a lawyer with unfounded complaints. If you do, you might find your file in a box outside of his or her door, waiting for you to pick it up.*

• take action against your lawyer (see Chapter Ten).

Does Your Lawyer Control Events? Or Do Events Control Your Lawyer. . . .

All of us at one time or another feel swept up by the "tides of life" over which we seem to have little or no control. This feeling of helplessness is bad enough when it occurs in our daily lives, but it can be devastating—sort of a personal San Francisco earthquake—when it occurs during a lawsuit.

In many respects, the tides of your lawsuit will be set during the transaction of events known as the "facts of the case," which occur *before going to court.* Part of your lawyer's job is to *predict* where these currents will lead. Thus, if these facts seem to be in your favor, your lawyer will want to "go with the flow." But, if they aren't, your lawyer's job is to try to "control the flow," to make it change direction. If that is not possible, then your lawyer's job, at the very least, is to do his or her best to make your situation as palatable as possible.

So, how does a lawyer control events? *Anticipation.* Your lawyer needs to be like a good chess player, that is, he or she must think *defensively* as well as *offensively*— and he or she must think several moves ahead.

Here are some storm warnings that tell you your lawyer is not in control:

You get hit by a "tidal wave" that your lawyer did not see coming.

This isn't the same thing as you losing a case. Even the very best lawyers at their very best lose cases. It means being adversely affected by events your lawyer should have seen and prepared for, but didn't.

The following conversation illustrates what I mean:

DEAD DUCK: *"What do you think my chances are?"*

LAWYER: *"Not good. First, the grocery clerk will testify that he saw you eat all of the cookies in the package, and then put the package back on the shelf. Second, there were crumbs all over your face when you were arrested. Third, I doubt whether the jury will believe your story about the wind blowing the crumbs onto your face right after you put on suntan oil."*

Obviously, this lawyer sees what's coming. His main job now is to try to reduce the consequences to his client.

Here's another example:

HOLLY HOPEFUL: *"Will I win?"*

LAWYER: *"I think so. But there is a chance that the judge will believe your former husband's testimony. If that happens, you could lose custody. So, I subpoenaed his psychiatrist to testify, just in case."*

The lawyer feels good about the case, but does see a potential problem and is prepared to meet it. (The client may still lose—that risk exists in every case—but at least the loss is likely to be because of the facts, and not lawyer error.)

Compare the above situations to the following "tidal wave":

UP A CREEK: *"Why didn't you tell me I could lose $50,000? You told me the worst that could happen was I'd have to pay $5,000 in costs!"*

LAWYER: *"I can't believe the jury believed that widow's lies. And those orphans! I mean, talk about a motley crew!"*

UP A CREEK: *"Why didn't you know they would testify?"*

LAWYER: *"What do you think I am, a psychic?"*

Now, this client got hit by events her lawyer didn't even see coming. If your lawyer has a habit of being surprised, you might be in a lot of trouble.

Your lawyer acts like a 90-pound weakling.
I'm not talking about physical strength. (I'm six feet tall and close to 200 lbs., and the first case I lost was to a lawyer who weighed 110 lbs.)

What I am talking about is *strength of personality.* If your lawyer seems afraid, in awe of his or her opponent or simply overwhelmed, you might have picked the wrong lawyer.

HINT: *Lawsuits are very much like wars—the tides of battle ebb and flow. One day you're on top, the next you're running for your life, planning a counter-attack. If, however, you feel like you're the Polish Cavalry against the Germans' tanks, you may need to bring in reinforcements.*

HINT: *Pay particular attention to your lawyer's performance in a deposition. Depositions are the trench warfare of lawsuits, where the force of a lawyer's personality can frequently mean the difference between success and failure.*

Does Your Lawyer Appear To Have A Solid Grasp Of The Case?

Lawsuits are really just high stakes arguments. And as any debator will tell you, the person who controls the definitions will win the debate.

Part of a lawyer's job is to seek to define the case in terms most favorable to his or her client. The only way your lawyer can hope to "define the issues" is to have a thorough grasp of the facts—and the law. If it appears that your lawyer *doesn't*—that he or she is in deep water—*you* may be the one who drowns.

Does Your Lawyer Give You Options?

Throughout the course of your legal problem, you will be faced with making choices to sue or not to sue—to settle or to fight—to accept or appeal. And to make matters a little more complex, there isn't a "right" answer, there are only options. Your lawyer's job is to present them all to you, to give you a recommendation, and then allow you to decide.

HINT: *If your lawyer doesn't present you with several options to choose from when asking you to make a decision, you probably don't have all of the information you need to make an* intelligent *decision.*

Does Your Lawyer Know The Strengths And Weaknesses Of Your Case?

I've said it several times before, and I'm going to say it again: *Every* case has its strengths and its weaknesses. If your lawyer isn't able to list *both* for you, the "soft underbelly" of your case may be exposed. And you won't even know it until you feel the sting of your opposition's teeth as he or she prepares to "eat you alive."

Do You Feel Good?

How do you feel about the case? Is your "sixth sense" telling you that something is wrong? If so, listen to your inner voice and then try to find the facts behind the feelings. Write yourself a letter, if necessary, to get your brain to express the problem. It can start out something like this: "I feel uncomfortable about my case because. . . ." Your answer may surprise you!

As you can see, *staying involved* in your own case should go a long way toward making your experience with your lawyer a beneficial one. But if it doesn't, and you feel you've received the thistles instead of the fruit, you will have descended into every client's worst nightmare—disputes with your own lawyer.

10
WHEN BEST LAID PLANS GO AWRY
WHAT TO DO IF YOU HAVE A DISPUTE WITH YOUR LAWYER

WRONG

I THINK IT'S TIME WE HAD A TALK...

RIGHT

If you are unhappy with your lawyer, you probably feel like Julius Caesar must have when his beloved Brutus made the final cut—furious that you've been betrayed, yet scared that you're going to die. Luckily, unlike Julius Caesar, you have a fighting chance. So here are some of the things you can do.

TALK TO YOUR LAWYER

Before you take any of the more drastic action available to you, try the "let us reason together" approach—by simply talking. After all, talk is more effective than making faces—and more mature than name-calling. And you just might be surprised how easily things can be worked out.

But, *before you talk, prepare.* Remember, your lawyer lives in a world of logic and evidence—where emotions are suppressed, and "may the best man win." So, you must approach your lawyer in a calm and businesslike manner. Don't worry, you can do it! Here's how . . .

- **Avoid emotionalism**
  Now, I realize that you are probably upset, but it does you no good to make unfounded emotional attacks such as "You're obviously on my husband's side—the rat! How much did he have to pay you to buy you off?!" Remember, your lawyer doesn't think of him- or herself as the "bad guy," and if you challenge his or her integrity, you will only make things worse than they already are.

- **Be specific**
  If you are unhappy, your lawyer has a right to know why—it isn't good enough to say "because." So you must be specific about the problems you are experiencing. This is why it is helpful to keep a Duplicate File Notebook. The evidence will be there in black and white (or blue and white, depending on the color pen you use). So, if your complaint is that your lawyer continually misses deadlines, be ready to give examples of when such omissions occurred.

- **Use notes**
  Lawyers usually have the "gift of gab"—so, if you try to talk with your lawyer *without notes,*

you may soon find yourself talking about "the chances of the Cubs reaching the World Series," rather than the fact that your lawyer did not mail that important letter as he or she promised. So bring in notes which list your complaints, and don't leave until they've all been resolved to your satisfaction—or until you come to the realization that you want to try name-calling after all.

- **Listen**
Most disputes occur because of faulty communication. So, as your lawyer explains his or her side of the story, listen with an open mind. You may learn things you somehow missed.

- **Take notes**
Write down what your lawyer tells you. In that way, you will always have a record of the conversation, in case you need it later. (For example if you are getting a second opinion.)

- **Get a second opinion**
You and your lawyer may not resolve your differences. If the dispute is regarding the quality of his or her performance, don't be afraid to get a second (or third) opinion. You may find that your lawyer was *right* all along!

- **Write a letter**
If your lawyer has a very strong personality which makes you feel somewhat intimidated, write a letter setting forth your complaints, and mail it to him or her *before* you talk. In that way you will be sure to "get everything off your chest" *without interruption*. And you can take all the time you want, to say all that you want to say. Remember to keep the letter polite, businesslike and to the point. Here's an example:

July 8th 19____
Mr. Horse's Butt
Attorney at Law
444 Make Excuses Place
Beaumont, Texas

Dear Mr. Butt,

The purpose of this letter is to complain about the poor service I believe I am receiving from you. I also write in the hope that the problems I see with the case can be resolved. Specifically, I have the following complaints:

1. On March 5th you promised me you would write my former employer to see what help he could be to my case. I talked to him yesterday and he says he hasn't received your letter. I double-checked the address I gave you (see my letter to you dated March 1st), and it is correct. Why haven't you written that letter?*

2. On May 2nd, you overcharged me for the court appearance. As you will recall, I was charged for four hours' time, yet for three of those four hours, you worked on other files while we waited our turn in court. I enclose a copy of your letter to me promising to adjust my bill. I also enclose the bills I have received from you since then—none of which correct the problem.**

3. You have not returned my last three phone calls. I realize you are busy, but I must demand the courtesy of a response, even if it is only to arrange a time for us to talk.

May we please meet within the next week to deal with these issues. Our future business relationship depends on it.

Thank you for your cooperation.

Very truly yours,

A. Sertive

This is an example of how letter writing can help you, should a problem arise. The letter this client mailed about his former employer's address now constitutes proof that the lawyer had the information he needed to take the promised action.

**Whenever possible, be it in a letter or an office visit, bring tangible proof to back up your complaint.*

After you have discussed the problems with your lawyer, *always write a confirming letter,* whether the dispute was resolved or not. Here's an example from the same client to the same lawyer.

> July 20th 19____
> Mr. Horse's Butt
> Attorney at Law
> 444 Make Excuses Place
> Beaumont, Texas

Dear Mr. Butt,

Thank you for meeting with me regarding the problems I wrote to you about on July 8th. As you will recall, we agreed upon the following:

1. That you would contact my former boss immediately. I called him today, and I was happy to learn that you and he talked at length about the case. I look forward to learning the details of your discussion.

2. That my bill will be adjusted as per your promise. Let's hope the computer gets it right this time.*

3. I accept your apology regarding the telephone calls, and I must admit that my calling you three times in four hours was a little much. I think it's a good idea to use your secretary as a go-between when you aren't in the office, so from now on, I'll leave a message or write a letter if you are unavailable.

I am happy we resolved our differences.

> Thank you,
>
> *A. Sertive*

---

*Lawyers always *blame the computer—but then, doesn't everyone?*

If your differences cannot be resolved, you have two choices: *live with it* or *take action*. Here are the options available to you if you choose the latter.

FIRE YOUR LAWYER

If you feel like the relationship with your lawyer can be compared to "the irresistible force meeting the immovable object," well the time has probably come to make new arrangements. This is not a step to be taken lightly, after all, a lot is at stake, but if you proceed in a proper and timely fashion (by not waiting till the last minute), you should be able to change lawyers with minimal harm to your case.

Trouble In Paradise

Only you can tell when the time has come to "fall back ten and punt." But, just as in football, there are some general guidelines you can follow which tell you that you are at "4th down and 8 to go" (in other words, you are going nowhere, fast).

- **Has your lawyer lost your trust?**
  If the relationship with your lawyer can be compared to owning a car, then trust is the oil that keeps it running smoothly. Take away the trust, and you're going to have a major breakdown. So, if that noise you hear is your engine dropping onto the middle of the road—the time has probably come to trade in your old clunker for a new model. At least you'll get better mileage.

- **Has your lawyer lost your confidence?**
  While trust has to do with *personal qualities*, confidence deals with *legal ability*—there *is* a difference. After all, even the most saintly lawyer can be incompetent. Or, as is more often the case, just the wrong lawyer for the task at hand. So, if your knight in shining armor now seems dented and tarnished, maybe you should find a new warrior to champion your cause.

- **Are you scared of your lawyer?**
  If you feel like Tokyo to your lawyer's Godzilla, then there is just no way for you and your lawyer to have an effective relationship. So, if your lawyer roars rather than listens, and breathes fire rather than talks, "don't fight—switch." After all, with a lawyer like that, who needs enemies?

- **Are you unable to communicate with your lawyer?**

  Effective communication is the heart of a good attorney/client relationship. Without it, you'll both seem lost at sea. So, if you feel like you are on a raft adrift in the ocean, with a lawyer who only speaks Swahili—cast off! That relationship isn't going anywhere.

- **Does your case have that "run down" feeling?**

  Sometimes a case just seems to get the "blahs." There's no major disaster, your lawyer seems to be trustworthy and competent, yet you still feel like the earth is slowly slipping away beneath your feet. Sometimes under such circumstances, "new blood" can make a big difference. So, if your instincts tell you your case needs a shot of adrenaline that your lawyer doesn't seem to offer, try looking elsewhere.

The Impact On Your Case Of Firing Your Lawyer

Changing lawyers is not a minor office procedure, it is major surgery and will have an impact on your case. Part of your job is to make sure that the pain is worth the benefit.

- **The financial impact**

  Hourly Fee Cases—In an hourly fee case, there is simply no way to avoid spending money that would not have been spent had you kept the same lawyer. Remember, your new lawyer will have to meet with you and read the file, so he or she can get educated about the facts in your case. This, by definition, takes time, which you pay for. So, be sure to ask your new lawyer how much he or she expects this "education" to cost *before* you sign up.

HINT: *If you come to the conclusion that you are going to fire your lawyer, don't procrastinate. Remember, the longer you take, the more work your current lawyer will have done, thus, the more your new lawyer's education will cost.*

HINT: *Just because you owe your first lawyer money, that doesn't mean you can't fire him or her. But don't be surprised if you are immediately pressured for payment. So, try to work out a deal beforehand. However, if you feel strongly that your former lawyer's work (or lack thereof) doesn't warrant payment, be prepared for a fight, because if you don't pay, you're likely to get sued.*

Contingency Fee Cases—If you change lawyers in a contingency fee case, make sure your new Retainer Agreement provides that any money your second lawyer is entitled to comes out of the "lawyer's percentage" of the money collected. In other words, you should only have to pay *one* contingency fee (be it 33% or 40% or whatever), *not two.*

HINT: *Lawyers frequently squabble with each other in such cases over what percentage of the contingency fee each is entitled to. That is their fight, not yours. You just have to make sure that you only pay one fee.*

- **The impact on the progress of your case**
  Your case will probably be put on hold for a short period of time while the new team takes

over. Thus, don't be surprised if your new lawyer asks for a short delay in a court hearing, deposition or other previously scheduled event. Remember, your new lawyer needs time to become familiar with the file. And besides, he or she may already have previous commitments.

- **The impact on the quality of the work**
  Obviously, clients change lawyers so that the quality of the work performed on their behalf will be improved. But there are dangers. For example, if you wait until the last minute, your lawyer may be forced into action, before he or she is fully prepared—which could prove to be disastrous. So, once you decide to switch, be sure to do it quickly. Every minute counts when a new lawyer is taking over a case that is already in progress.

HINT: *It is especially dangerous to change lawyers just before trial. Your new lawyer may believe he or she can get a "continuance" (a delay) in the proceeding, but the judge may not agree. And the judge is definitely a "majority of one" where such matters are concerned.*

- **The impact on your life**
  If you are changing lawyers, you are going to have to invest a great deal of time and effort—not only in finding the "right" lawyer, but in making the transition work. This cannot help but affect your personal life. So, if you are not prepared to make the sacrifice, don't change lawyers.

- **The impact on your reputation with the court**
  Officially there should be none. But in the real world, lawyers and judges take special note of clients who go from lawyer to lawyer to lawyer. The impact can be subtle, and impossible to prove (like a judge not believing your testimony because he or she has decided you are a "flake" before he or she ever sees you). Or, it could be less subtle (like a judge forcing a new lawyer to trial before he or she is fully prepared). So, when you decide to change lawyers, choose your lawyer carefully. Because if you switch more than one or two times, you may find yourself "behind the 8 ball" before you even get to present your case.

HINT: *This "flake" reputation can be most damaging during chambers conferences. Chambers conferences are meetings between the judge and the lawyers—out of the presence of the parties (you). They are usually over procedural items, like deciding what will happen when. But sometimes, especially in courts with congested calendars, they deal with matters of substance. It is on those occasions that an opposition lawyer may try to discredit you, by pointing out that you "change lawyers the way most people change clothing." This charge may be enough to tip the scale against you in a close decision. So again,* try to choose your lawyer wisely.

How To Fire Your Lawyer

Most people avoid personal confrontations the way cats avoid water. But don't worry, it won't be so bad. And, if you follow my suggestions, hopefully you won't even end up in a shouting match where you are yelling, "You're fired!" and your lawyer is countering with, "You can't fire me, I QUIT!"

The easiest method of firing your lawyer is to have your new lawyer do it for you. All you do is sign a form. Your new lawyer will take the responsibility of notifying his or her predecessor and arranging for the transfer of the file.

HINT: *Treat this transaction as you do all others in the case—ask your new lawyer when the transfer will take place, and put the date in your calendar so that you can follow up. You should also ask for copies of any form you sign (usually called a "Substitution of Attorney"), and any letters that may be sent between your former lawyer and your new one. It's that simple.*

If, however, you believe you must get rid of your old attorney quickly, you should inform your lawyer (by phone if you want) of your decision. If things have gone this far, don't waste your time in discussing the reasons for your action. You will just be rehashing old business. Make it simple and to the point.

> CLIENT: *"Joe, I've decided I don't require your services anymore, and I want to pick up my file. When can you have it ready?"*
>
> LAWYER: *"But, why? I thought we'd worked things out."*
>
> CLIENT: *"I just think it's best. When can I pick up my file?"*
>
> LAWYER: *"Today at 3:00."*
>
> CLIENT: *"Thank you, I'll be there."*

HINT: *If your lawyer is unavailable, leave the same message with his or her secretary, and call back later to find out when you can pick up the file. Be sure to send a confirming letter.*

If you prefer, you can take the action by mail, instead of in person or by phone. Here is a sample letter:

May 4, 19____
Ms. Past Tense
Attorney at Law
8686 Hit the Road Ave.
San Francisco, CA

Dear Ms. Tense,

After careful consideration, I have decided that your services are no longer required. Thus, would you please have my file ready for me to pick up by May 8th? I will be by on that date at 3:00 PM.

Would you also get whatever forms are necessary for me to sign to make myself my own attorney, and take the responsibility of filing them with the court? Of course I will want a copy for my records.

Thank you for your cooperation.

Best,

Ms. On My Own

If your legal matter involves a court case, be sure your old lawyer prepares the Substitution of Attorney, and whatever other forms may be necessary to make you your own lawyer (in lawyerese, that's Propria Personae—or Pro Per for short). Your old lawyer should prepare the documents for you and have them properly filed—with copies sent to the other side.

HINT: *Until such forms are properly processed, your lawyer still has official responsibility for your case. Don't be afraid to ask exactly what the correct procedure is. After all, most lawyers get fired occasionally—it comes with the territory—so he or she probably won't be too upset. Just be sure you get copies for your file—and give them to your new lawyer when you find one.*

HINT: *If you are not involved in a court case, a Substitution of Attorney is probably not necessary. But be sure to notify anyone involved with the matter, so that all future communication can be made directly to you.*

Find your new lawyer *fast*. When you are in Pro Per, you are expected to comply with all of the rules and procedures that a lawyer must. So don't waste time in finding your old lawyer's replacement. Otherwise, you may find that you have bitten off more than you can chew.

If you feel your lawyer has literally "hurt you", you may want to take the next step, which is to. . . .

SUE YOUR LAWYER

Lawyers and doctors have traditionally been at each other's throats, but they do have at least one thing in common—they *both* can be sued for malpractice.

Examples Of Lawyer Negligence

Suing is easy! It's winning that's hard! That's because you have to prove *two* cases: *first*, the lawyer's malpractice, and (in most cases), *second*, that you *would have won* the original case if the lawyer had *not* botched it up! No easy task.

Malpractice is just another word for negligence. But negligence doesn't mean losing a case, or even making a tactical error. It means conduct below the "standards of practice for lawyers in the community." And who, you ask, can tell you whether that has occurred? Yup, other lawyers. So, like it or not, if you sue your lawyer for malpractice, you can expect to be hip-deep in attorneys for the duration of the case.

Of course, some conduct is almost by definition malpractice. Here is a partial list.

- **Filing a lawsuit after the Statute Of Limitations has expired**
  All civil suits have a time limit within which they *must* be filed. And, if your lawyer is even one day late, you *lose by forfeit.* If your lawyer allowed this to happen to you (assuming you gave him or her accurate information and

enough time to prepare a suit), he or she has probably committed malpractice.

> **HINT:** *Ask your lawyer if your case has a Statute of Limitations, and write it down. Then make sure your case is filed in the court before that date.*

- **Failing to prosecute or defend your case, which results in a verdict against you**
  There are all sorts of time limits your lawyer works under. In California, for example, a civil case must be brought to trial within five years of its filing—or it must be dismissed. (Time limits vary from state to state, so ask your lawyer about the law in your jurisdiction.) Other such rules include time limits within which to serve process, file briefs or conduct discovery. The idea here is that if you lose because of technical or procedural failures on the part of your lawyer (through no fault of your own), he or she probably committed malpractice.

- **Failing to name the right party in a suit or a cross complaint—or failure to serve the right party**
  Sometimes lawyers do not name the right party when they sue someone on your behalf. I know of one case where a man was named in a civil suit (I'll call him Slimeball). Well, Slimeball was about fifty years old, but the process server served Slimeball Jr. who was about twenty-five. Luckily the attorney involved caught the mistake in time, and justice prevailed. But I . . . er, I mean *that* lawyer sure had sweaty palms for a while.

> **HINT:** *Always give your attorney a picture of someone you are going to sue—or at least a physical description. It may save your lawyer from making a serious mistake.*

Other common cases of malpractice are more difficult to prove. They include:

- failure to call a key witness at trial
- poor trial preparation
- suing under the wrong legal theory
- poor trial tactics
- breach of confidentiality
- failure to advise of probable tax consequences
- giving the wrong advice
- failure to anticipate pending changes in statutory or case law*

The Rest Of The Task

Assuming you get over the first hurdle, and can prove your lawyer's conduct was negligent—you're still only halfway home. You have to prove you suffered damages as a result of the malpractice. That usually means you have to prove what is termed "the underlying case." For example, if your lawyer blew an accident case, you have to completely prove that you would have won the case (as well as prove the malpractice), or you don't win one penny.

Or, if your lawyer gave you the wrong tax advice, you have to prove you paid unnecessary taxes as a result. In short, you win *only* when you can prove you lost money,

Lawyers have a duty to keep up with the ever-changing landscape of the law. Some lawyers have actually lost malpractice cases for failing to predict future appellate court decisions. Now, obviously, I can't name every example of lawyer malpractice that has ever existed, but I think you get the idea.

time (such as time spent in jail) or opportunity—or suffered significant emotional trauma which you would not have "but for" the lawyer's negligence. Like I said, no easy task.

The importance of the Duplicate File Notebook
With such a burden placed upon you, it is obvious that you will need all of the evidence you can get to back up your contentions. That is part of the reason I urge you to keep your own file—so that you will be able to recreate the events that occurred during your case—even years afterwards.*

CAVEAT:

This constitutes a mere "scratching of the surface" of the subject of malpractice. *It is not a substitute for, nor does it attempt to give legal advice.* So, if you feel you have suffered damages as a result of your lawyer's negligence, *see a malpractice attorney* (yes, they exist) *about the specifics of your case.*

Fee Arbitrations

The "fly" that most often spoils the ointment of the attorney-client relationship is not malpractice, but fee disputes. These difficulties used to end up in court, but there is a movement now in many states to resolve them outside of the court system, through the use of State Bar-sponsored arbitrations. Here are the benefits of such arbitrations to you:

- You may not need to hire a lawyer, especially if you have kept accurate records.
- The formalities of court procedures are dispensed with in favor of an informal atmosphere.

Of course, the most important reason I urge you to maintain the notebook is to make sure malpractice doesn't happen at all!

- The dispute can be resolved relatively quickly.
- The emphasis is on a fair resolution of the dispute, rather than winning or losing.
- If your lawyer has sued you, some states will "stay" (suspend) the court case until the arbitration can be held.

If your State Bar Association has a program of arbitrations, take advantage of it, should the need arise. If it doesn't, write to your State Bar Association and ask them to provide the service. They are an excellent form of dispute resolution. (See the supplement at the end of this book to see if your state has a fee arbitration program available to you.)

If your lawyer's misconduct involved UNETHICAL CONDUCT, you can. . . .

REPORT YOUR LAWYER

Reporting your lawyer to the State Bar Association is a very serious step and should only be taken under the most serious of circumstances. There are two excellent reasons for this: *first,* a relatively trivial matter will not result in your lawyer being disciplined. *Second,* and more important, it will waste the time of Bar investigators, whose resources are already near the breaking point in many states.

Here is a sample of lawyer misconduct that should be reported:

- stealing client property
- negligently losing client property
- breaking client confidences
- failing to disclose conflicts of interest

- abandoning a client's case
- lying about lawyer's performance or covering up
- failure to perform
- refusing to communicate with client
- incompetence
- co–mingling client and lawyer assets

If your lawyer engages in any of the above mis-conduct—report him or her, even if you were not injured. After all, that lawyer's next client might not be so lucky.

Here is a sample of a letter reporting a lawyer to a State Bar Association. Always send copies of documents which back up your allegations. And always give your lawyer's full name and office address. Be as specific as you can when outlining the misconduct.

September 11, 19____
State Bar Association of California
555 Franklin Street
San Francisco, CA 94102

Regarding: Unprofessional conduct of
Peter S. Cad, Attorney at Law

To Whom It May Concern;

On July 7th, I hired Peter S. Cad, whose office is located at 444 Crooked Guy Lane, Santa Monica, CA, to represent me in a lawsuit against a building contractor. I paid a $1,000 Retainer, and agreed to pay $150 an hour (enclosed is a copy of the Retainer Agreement).

Mr. Cad promised me he would file a lawsuit within two weeks. When I had not heard from him after that time, I called him. He assured me that the paperwork was being processed. The week after that, on July 26th to be exact, I called Mr. Cad asking for a copy of the Complaint. When I had not received it by August, I wrote Mr. Cad a letter requesting a copy of all of the work he had performed on my behalf (copy enclosed). I never received a response.

I have since hired a new lawyer and asked Mr. Cad for a return of my $1,000. He refuses, claiming he is entitled to the money under the Retainer Agreement.

I believe Mr. Cad should be prevented from treating clients in this shameful way. I would also like you to help me get my $1,000 back.

My home address is: 8862 Victim Road
My home phone is: (213)888-8888
My work phone is: (213)444-4444 *

Your prompt response will be appreciated.

Sincerely,

Very Upset

Once you have reported your lawyer to the Bar, an investigator will be assigned to your case, and an investigation will be held to determine whether discipline is

Always include a phone number where you can be contacted during business hours.

warranted. Be sure to use your Duplicate File Notebook to back up your story—after all, your lawyer's very livelihood is at stake, so the Bar Association will want compelling proof of misconduct.

> **HINT:** *The length of time it takes for the investigation to be conducted, and the procedures of the investigation itself, vary widely from state to state. Ask the investigator assigned to your case for the specifics in your jurisdiction.*

If your lawyer is found to have engaged in misconduct, he or she will be disciplined. This discipline can range from disbarment (revocation of the license to practice law) to suspension (loss of license for a specific period of time) to reprimand (no loss of license, but a declaration that the lawyer engaged in misconduct). A disciplined lawyer can also be ordered to pay you restitution costs, as well as engage in educational courses or other forms of discipline that may be appropriate.

> **HINT:** *Lawyers can also be disciplined for improper conduct that has nothing to do with their clients, but is beyond the scope of this book. If you would like more information, contact your State Bar Association.*

Client Security Funds

If you have lost money because of lawyer misconduct, you may be able to recover all or part of your loss. Most State Bar Associations maintain a client security fund to reimburse clients who have lost money at their own lawyer's hands. For details in your state, contact your State Bar Association. (You, of course, also have the right to sue for malpractice in addition to seeking to have your lawyer disciplined.)

11

GOD HELPS THOSE WHO HELP THEMSELVES

WHEN YOU CAN GO IT ALONE

In the "simple days of yore," the average person rarely had to use lawyers (perhaps that is why they were so respected). But today all that has changed. In fact, life (and the legal system) has become so complicated that legal problems which can be handled *without* using a lawyer may soon be added to the Endangered Species List. But they still do exist, so let's take a look at them before they become museum pieces.

SMALL CLAIMS COURT

Judge Wapner here we come! If you've watched *The People's Court* on television, you've seen small claims court in action. Small claims matters are civil cases in which the amount of money in dispute is relatively low— usually less than $1,500 (see your local court rules for the specifics in your jurisdiction). The litigants (a big word for the "suer" and the "suee") represent themselves— each telling a judge their side of the story. The case moves quickly (there are no lawyers involved), with as many as thirty or forty cases being heard a day. If your dispute is small, there are several reasons to take it to small claims court:

- **Speed**
  Your case will be resolved in a matter of weeks, or at the most, a few months.

- **Convenience**
  Your case will be heard quickly at a court near your home.

- **Economy**
  No lawyer's fees. Costs which rarely exceed $25.00.

Generally, here's how the process works (specific procedures may differ in your jurisdiction).

A person who believes he or she is owed money (the plaintiff) goes to the local small claims court and asks the court clerk for the forms necessary to file a case (usually a Summons and a Complaint.) The forms are simple, and the plaintiff fills them out in full.

The forms are then handed to the clerk, along with a small filing fee. The clerk checks to make sure they have been filled out correctly, and if they have, the original is used to open the court file—at least one copy is given back to the plaintiff, and *a trial date is set*, which appears on the paper.

The plaintiff takes the Summons and Complaint to the local Sheriff's Office or U.S. marshal to make arrangements to have it served. (Ask the court clerk whom to see.)

HINT: *Service must be done within a time limit. The form will tell you what that limit is.*

At the marshal's office, the plaintiff prepares the forms necessary for the marshal to serve the person sued (the defendant). A small fee is charged to serve the defendant.

HINT: *Generally, you are* not *allowed to serve the defendant yourself. You can have a friend do it, but if one does, he or she must fill out a "proof of service" form.*

Once the marshal has served the defendant, you will receive a document known as a "proof of service" in the mail. This is a written declaration under penalty of perjury which names the person served, the date and the time of day. *Be sure you bring it to court with you.* If the defendant is a "no show," you will not be able to present your case without it.

If you are a defendant and you received such a lawsuit, you too must go visit your friendly court clerk. There you will be given forms to fill out, denying you owe any money. (You can also counter-sue the plaintiff if the amount *you* want is not over the amount of the small claims court jurisdiction.) A copy of your answer must be sent to the plaintiff.

When the day for trial arrives, be sure to be on time, because if you are not, they will probably proceed without you.

At trial, the plaintiff tells his or her side of the story first, followed by the defendant. Here are some hints to help you do a good job:

- Prepare before you go to trial. Write down everything you think is important and take your notes with you so you do not forget anything.
- Take notes about what the other party is saying. Underline the things you wish to dispute when your turn comes, so that you don't forget.
- Be polite. You are in a court of law, so . . .
- Don't interrupt (you'll get your turn). Don't act rudely, you may turn the judge against you.
- Bring proof. Documents can always be submitted as evidence, and witnesses can usually be called. So, bring as much evidence as you have to prove your point.

After your case is over, the judge may tell you the verdict—or you may be notified by mail.

IF YOU LOSE, you can:

- File an Appeal. Ask the court clerk for the forms and follow the instructions.

> **HINT:** *Lawyers are usually permitted to participate in small claims appeals, so, if you feel strongly about your appeal, think about bringing in "the big gun" (a lawyer). However, be aware that appeals are hard to win.*

- See if you can pay in monthly payments— *sometimes* this is permitted.

IF YOU WIN, you can:

- Contact the defendant and arrange for payment.

> **HINT:** *If the defendant refuses to pay, you have the right to enforce the Judgment legally. This can get complicated, and you should seriously consider hiring a lawyer at this point.*

> **HINT:** *Some lawyers specialize in "collection cases," and will work on a percentage basis. If you can't find such a lawyer, see a collection agency (they usually will). Just be sure to bring a certified copy of your Judgment with you.*

TRAFFIC COURT

People rarely hire lawyers to fight traffic tickets. The key to winning in traffic court is rebutting the police officer's testimony. This is usually done with witnesses, pictures or compelling testimony. Fighting a ticket is difficult, and should only be attempted if you truly are innocent, and can honestly testify under oath "I didn't do it." Otherwise, you have two chances of winning—*slim* and *none*. I know of what I speak; the following is a case in point . . .

I was sitting as a judge pro-tem in traffic court, when a very angry man who had received a ticket for making a right turn without signalling appeared before me. He was convinced he could "beat" his ticket because the officer had mistakenly put down the *wrong name* of a street the defendant had been driving on, before he made the turn. After he finished his dissertation, he stated he expected to be found "not guilty" because the policeman had made an error. "Interesting theory," I said, "but *did you signal* when you turned right?" (After all, that is what he was charged with—making a right hand turn without signaling.) His answer was "No." I had to find him guilty.

Notes about traffic court

The court is usually run on a formal basis. In other words, there is a prosecuting attorney, with examination and cross-examination of witnesses.

Police officers are what I call "professional witnesses"—testifying is part of their job—and they are GOOD at it! (Even when they lie, er, I mean "exaggerate"—it *does* happen.) So, prepare your cross-examination and practice it before you come to court. (Again, write down what you want to say ahead of time.)

Even though, technically, the prosecutor is supposed to prove you guilty "beyond a reasonable doubt," in real life a "tie" usually goes to the police officer. So try to provide more of a case than "It's your word against mine."

If you take the stand in your own defense, be prepared to be cross-examined by an "expert"—the prosecuting attorney.

Most jurisdictions offer an alternative to paying a traffic ticket, by permitting some defendants, under certain conditions, to go to "traffic school." If you qualify, it does cost money, but the ticket doesn't go on your record. Ask the court clerk whether traffic school is an alternative available in your jurisdiction.

You can use a lawyer if you want to—and probably *should* if a conviction would cause you to suffer more than the usual fine (consequences such as jail time or a cancellation of your automobile insurance).

SIMPLE WILLS

If your estate (your assets) is small, you may want to write your own will. (My personal belief is that you should hire a lawyer, as the preparation of a simple will is usually relatively inexpensive.) There are many books available which can help you (none of which I have read, so I can't recommend one), but I strongly suggest you buy one so that you can learn the formalities.

By the way, some states now provide "fill in the blank" form wills, for use in restricted circumstances. If your state does, I strongly suggest you buy the forms rather than trying to "wing it" yourself.

MINOR TRAFFIC ACCIDENTS

If you are involved in an accident involving *property damage* (not personal injury), you can probably negotiate a settlement without using a lawyer. Remember the following.

- You will need to prove the amount of your loss. Get at least *three estimates from reputable body shops* before settling.
- Choose a body shop the responsible insurance company approves of. Then, later, if there is a problem, you have two places to go, to seek to correct it: the body shop, and the insurance company.

- If the insurance company decides to "total" your car (pay you the "book" value), and you think that the amount is too low, you can sometimes get your way by cutting ads out of the classified section of a newspaper, which show a car like yours selling for a higher price. Also, if your car had unusual and valuable accessories, be sure to mention them— they may entitle you to more money.

PURCHASE OF A HOME

Many people don't use a lawyer to negotiate the purchase or sale of a home, they either do it themselves or hire real estate agents or brokers. Frankly, I think this is a mistake. After all, buying or selling a home is one of the biggest contracts most of us will ever enter into.

If you use a real estate agent/broker, remember:

- Their commission is usually negotiable.
- They *are* (unlike lawyers) allowed to "represent" *both* the buyer and the seller. This can lead to problems. So, if you are the buyer, I strongly suggest you get your own agent. Especially since the seller normally pays the commission (which is split by the agents).

- When agents advise you, remember, their liveli-hood *depends* on that sale going through (otherwise they don't get paid). So, if you have any doubts about the advice given, please consult a lawyer.

- *Some* real estate professionals are "weekend agents" who know just enough to pass a test (and just enough to get you into trouble). So, if you decide to use an agent, *check out their credentials before you sign a contract of representation.* And, as with lawyers, don't use an agent *just because* he or she is your friend. There's just too much at stake.

HINT: *Listing or Representation Agreements that you sign with a real estate agent or broker* are contracts, *and can be enforced as such. So, make sure you understand all of the terms (along with any fine print) before you sign. Remember, "act in haste—repent at leisure."*

Of course, legally you can represent yourself in any legal matter whatsoever. But, it's not usually a wise thing to do. So, let's look at some of the times when you really should get professional legal help.

12

PRIDE GOETH BEFORE A FALL

EXAMPLES OF WHEN YOU SHOULD HIRE A LAWYER

As a kid, I loved going to the movies on Saturday afternoons to watch Westerns. At some point in many of the films, usually during the second reel, the hero or his best friend would get shot, and a country doctor would be called to take out the bullet. There was no anesthesia, so our wounded cowboy would bite on a bullet wrapped in cloth to help him handle the pain.

Well, if you have a legal problem, you probably feel like that cowboy—you're wounded, you need help—but there is simply no way to avoid the pain and live. So, be smart, "bite the bullet" and hire yourself a lawyer.

Few people would defend themselves in a death penalty murder case—or try to sue General Motors for $10,000,000 without a lawyer. But many try to represent themselves in lesser cases, only to prove that the old adage, "He who represents himself, has a fool for a client," is true. So, here is a brief look at some circumstances where a lawyer is a virtual *must*.

THE PURCHASE OF A BUSINESS

When you buy a business, you are pursuing the "American Dream." But if you are not careful, it can easily turn into a nightmare. I know of a case where a man purchased a business without using a lawyer or a business broker. He purchased, among other things, the "goodwill" of the business, but he agreed to allow the seller to keep the business phone number and compete locally in the same business. Much to his surprise (and dismay), the income of the business dropped sharply soon after he took over. When the lawsuit happened (was there any doubt?) it turned out that the seller kept most of the business for himself. See, the business was mostly conducted by phone, so *the phone number was the goodwill!* (A business lawyer would have told him that.) The buyer not only had to spend thousands of dollars in attorneys' fees to bring the lawsuit, but he lost his house to foreclosure because he couldn't pay his bills.

This tragedy could probably have been avoided, if the unfortunate businessman had retained a lawyer. So, don't be "penny wise and pound foolish." If you are going to spend the money to buy a business—spend a little more for legal help. It's probably *deductible,* and it could literally be the difference between the good life and the poor farm.

DIVORCES

Have you been married more than two years? Have you obtained property during your marriage? Have you had children? If you say "yes" to even one of these questions, you owe it to yourself (and your children) at least to consult with a lawyer before you file for divorce or agree to a settlement.

Divorces used to be the backwater of legal practice—but no longer. Divorce law has become one of the most complex and fast-changing areas of law there is. Here is just a partial list of issues that may be part of a typical case:

Children
Who gets custody? What about visitation, support and medical care? And these are just the easy issues. You may also have to deal with tax deductions, religious training, birthdays, grandparent's rights and choice of schools.

Spousal Support (Alimony)

Should one spouse receive it? If so, for how long? And if one spouse has been at home, what about job training or higher education? And what are the tax implications?

Dividing the property

What is the marital property and what isn't? How much is it worth? Who gets what and why? Should the family home be sold? What about pension plans, how should they be divided? Is a professional license or a piece of property subject to division?

As you can see, divorces aren't what they used to be.

HINT: *Frequently a divorcing couple will try to use one lawyer to save money (or because one spouse pressures the other to do so). This can be a mistake. Lawyers are advocates, and under our adversary system, cannot represent two people with conflicting interests at the same time (and if divorcing couples aren't in conflict, who is?). The lawyer's loyalty must go to the person whom he or she officially represents. So, if you are the unrepresented party, be careful. You may not get the whole story.*

CRIMINAL CASES

If you know enough to come in out of the rain, you know enough to get a lawyer if you are charged with a *serious crime* (especially since one will be appointed for you if you can't afford to hire your own). But many people make the mistake of representing themselves in cases they view as minor, such as:

Petty Theft

The only thing "petty" about being charged with this crime is its name (because it usually involves less than $250 or so). The key word here is *theft*. And a conviction can bring severe and *lifelong* consequences, such as:

- You may be unable to become bonded.
- You may be disqualified from obtaining a professional license (such as a real estate license or a license to practice law).
- You may be prevented from getting a government job, and
- You will not be able to obtain a security clearance.

All these, not to mention the immediate consequences of a stiff fine, possible jail time and several years on probation.

Drunk Driving

It is hard to win a drunk driving case, even for lawyers. But it can be done. Even if you can't beat the case, you should have a lawyer represent you, because there are things which can be done for the guilty (such as occasionally having the charges reduced).

Some consequences of a conviction for drunk driving include:

- A stiff (and justified) fine
- Loss of your driving privilege
- Mandatory jail time in some states, especially upon a second conviction
- Auto insurance problems

Sex Crimes

Some "minor" sex crimes can lead to lifelong consequences. One of these is—being forced to "register"
yourself with the police as a "sexual deviate" wherever
you take up residence.

SPECIAL NOTE TO ALIENS

If you are an alien living in the United States, and you
are charged with any crime bigger than a traffic ticket,
consult a lawyer immediately! The consequences of being
convicted of even a minor crime can include deportation!

PERSONAL INJURY CASES

Personal injury cases usually pit the injured party
against insurance companies—which is sort of like
Woody Allen trying to outbox Muhammad Ali. Thus,
lawyers really are an unfortunate necessity in all but the
most minor of cases. They sort of even up the odds. Besides, good P.I. (Personal Injury) lawyers can do far more
than handle the legal aspects of your case. They can:

- Refer you to the right doctors.
- Convince doctors to defer payment until the case is
  settled.
- Work to resolve any property claims with the insurance company quickly and effectively.
- Advise you of the latest diagnostic and treating
  techniques.

MALPRACTICE CASES

The law of malpractice is growing increasingly complex, especially in the field of "medical mal" (as we call it in The Biz), where roadblocks are quickly being erected to make such lawsuits more difficult to file—and less lucrative to win. If you believe you have been injured by a professional's negligence, be it a doctor, lawyer, dentist, or even a real estate broker, consult a lawyer. You'll never make it on your own.

WILLS

As I stated in the last chapter, you may be able to write a simple will without a lawyer, but it's probably worth paying the modest price to have the will done right.

If your will is going to be complex, if it is going to contain a trust, if your assets are such that you will want to reduce estate taxes—use a lawyer. Your heirs will bless you, and you will rest easier in your grave if you do. Here are some other things you may want done in your will, which will require a lawyer's expertise:

- If you wish to provide "unusual" bequests in your will, such as, "I leave my '56 T-Bird to Cousin Wilbur to use during his years in college—and then to Aunt Nettie to use as a geranium planter."
- If you leave assets to a charity, a non-profit institution, to be used for a *specific purpose,* such as, "I leave $50,000 to Boys' Town for the erection of a statue in honor of the longest living boy of all, Peter Pan."
- If you wish to disinherit a close relative.
- If you have children from previous marriages or unions.

There are more, so if in doubt, confer with an attorney.

TRUSTS

Trusts come in all sizes, shapes and colors. They can be "inter vivos" (while you're alive) or, "testamentary" (if you're not). They can be revocable or irrevocable. They can be established so that a trusted third party manages the property—or so that you manage it yourself. In short, trusts are complicated and very technical in nature, so I advise against ever trying to create one without legal assistance.

CONSERVATORSHIPS AND GUARDIANSHIPS

If you wish to become the legal guardian of a minor, or take control of the person or property of an incompetent individual, you will have to go to court to do so. Always use a lawyer, because it's just too easy to make mistakes.

BANKRUPTCY

If your debts far exceed your assets, you may be considering bankruptcy. If you are, consult a lawyer first, because there may be another way out.

In some areas of the country, there are non-profit organizations which help debt-ridden individuals to work their way back into the sunlight without filing bankruptcy.

If you decide bankruptcy is the only way to go, I still say you need a lawyer even in the most simple cases. The forms are long and complex (I have handled a few bankruptcies for clients in my day, and it took me so long to fill out the darn forms, I wanted to hire a lawyer myself). Beyond convenience, a good bankruptcy lawyer will put an end to the collection agency threats, and the "notices to pay" very quickly, and can advise you of how to deal with secured creditors (those who have the right to foreclose on property if they are not paid). Also, bankruptcy is a very technical area of the law, and since you can only go bankrupt once in seven years, you don't want to make a mistake.

COLLECTION CASES

If you have a Judgment for money entered against you, a lawyer can help you prevent your creditor from taking all you own. So, if your wages have been attached, or your house is threatened with foreclosure, a lawyer may help you stem the tide.

If you are being hounded for debts you claim you do not owe—and talk has failed—consider hiring a lawyer. After all, he or she may not be as easy to push around.

INSURANCE CASES

Insurance policies are complicated contracts. If you believe you are entitled to receive benefits under your policy and your company refuses to pay—consult a lawyer.
Your company may be wrong. Besides, many states now
have laws which might permit you to sue your insurance
company for "bad faith" if their refusal to pay was not a
good faith error. Only a lawyer can tell you for sure.

HINT: *If you are sued for damages and have a liability policy—such as
that contained in a homeowners policy—bring it to your insurance agent's
attention. You may qualify to have your defense "on them."*

BUSINESS INVESTMENTS

If you are asked to invest in a limited partnership, a gold
mine or otherwise take large sums of your hard earned
cash and give it to a person or business as a tax shelter or
business investment, please talk to a good lawyer first
(especially if you are told "It's a sure thing.") Remember,
the proverbial Brooklyn Bridge comes in many shapes
and sizes.

HINT: *An honest business person will have no objection to discussing
the proposal with your lawyer, and allowing him or her to make a thorough
investigation before you invest. So, if you are rushed, or otherwise pressured, be extra careful.*

CAVEAT:

There are many other times when hiring a lawyer is a
wise path to follow, such as when obtaining a patent or
forming a public corporation. I have just tried to list
some of the more common areas of law where going it
alone is foolish. Don't forget "Fools rush in where wise
men never go."

13

"SAY WHAT?"
A SHORT COURSE IN LEGALESE

"IN THE EVENT OF BREACH, THE PARTY OF THE FIRST PART SHALL OWE THE PARTY OF THE SECOND PART 5,000 HEBREW SLAVES AND THREE NUBIAN DANCING GIRLS, AS LIQUIDATED DAMAGES."

(Translated from ancient Egyptian hieroglyphics, this is believed to be the first known example of legalese.)

As we can see, even in ancient times, lawyers had a language all their own. So, if you have problems understanding your lawyer, don't despair. You are merely carrying on one of man's most enduring traditions. However, if you are a nonconformist, and would actually like to understand what your lawyer tells you, this glossary of terms may help. So, here are some words commonly used by lawyers—with loose translations into "normal people's language."

Adverse Counsel—The S.O.B. who represents the other side.

Answer—A court document filed in court by someone who has been sued, which denies anything happened—and then states, "Even if it did, it wasn't my fault."

Appeal—What people do when they are unhappy with a trial court verdict. Often, a tactic to delay the inevitable.

Arbitration—A judicial proceeding which comes somewhere between a trial and a street brawl. Arbitrations are less formal than trials, but can be just as binding.

Arraignment—The court appearance where both the innocent and guilty alike plead "not guilty."

Attachment—What winners of lawsuits do to the loser's assets . . . sometimes known as the process of "squeezing blood out of a turnip."

Attorney–Client Privilege—That rule of law which protects the sanctity of the private communications between lawyer and client. (Frequently saving the client a lot of embarrassment.)

Bar Association—A club for lawyers where they gather to exchange information and sharpen teeth.

Breach of Contract—Changing your mind about keeping a promise made in a contract. Usually an expensive mistake. (see CONTRACT)

Brief—A written argument filed by lawyers which sets forth their version of the pertinent facts and law of a case. Briefs usually aren't.

Canon of Ethics—Regulations which keep lawyers honest; the violation of which usually leads to a "slap on the wrist."

Case Law—Published rulings issued by Appellate Courts which interpret statutes and other cases. Used by lawyers as guides for "splitting hairs."

Causes of Action—Found in civil complaints, usually in bunches. Each cause of action sets forth a different law which was allegedly violated by the person or entity being sued. Plaintiff's lawyers usually throw in everything but the kitchen sink.

Chambers Conference—When the lawyers and the judge meet behind closed doors to talk about the case and in which some clients wrongly feel they are being "sold down the river."

Client Trust Account—Where the lawyer holds your money before it is spent on your behalf . . . unless he or she is dishonest. (see CO-MINGLING)

Co-mingling—What dishonest lawyers do with your money and theirs, when they rob Peter to pay Paul.

Community Service—An alternative sentencing program, in which famous entertainers convicted of crimes put on shows instead of going to jail (and in which *you* are ordered to clean bed pans).

Complaint—The court pleading in a civil case which contains the suing party's tale of woe. Usually filled to the brim with Causes of Action. (see CAUSES OF ACTION)

Confidentiality—Your lawyer's duty to keep what you tell him or her in private, a secret. Often violated by lawyers when telling "war stories" with names not being used.

Conflict of Interest—Part of the Canon of Ethics that prevents your lawyer from handling your case while having an interest in conflict to your own. (Sorry, exhorbitant fees do not constitute a conflict of interest.)

Consideration—Something of value given in exchange for a promise which makes a contract binding. Also, something many people feel lawyers lack.

Contempt of Court—A willful violation of a lawful court order. Also, when a judge sentences you or your lawyer to jail for telling him or her what you *really* think.

Continuance—A delay in a court proceeding, usually because one of the lawyers is "engaged" elsewhere—or the case is not "ripe" for trial. Translation: the lawyers haven't done all of their work. (A major cause of court congestion.)

Contract—An agreement, whether written or oral, that the law will enforce. (Unless you are a star baseball player.)

Costs—The expenses incurred during a lawsuit other than for attorney's fees. Believed by some historians to be the original "bottomless pit."

Counsel—The fancy name lawyers call each other, as in "Go to hell, Counsel," "After you, Counsel."

Court Clerk—Underpaid, overworked bureaucrats who keep the courts functioning. The real powers that be—offend one at your own risk.

Cross-Complaint—A Complaint filed by the person being sued, against the suing party (or others, known as third parties), based on the old adage, "The best defense is a good offense."

Cross-Examination—The pleasant* process by which a lawyer challenges a witness's testimony.

Damages—What people who bring lawsuits claim they have suffered, usually in exaggerated terms.

Declaration—A written statement signed under penalty of perjury, which sets your version of the facts in concrete, and, if false, can sink you to the bottom of the litigation river.

Default—The legal equivalent to forfeiting a game for failure to appear. If default is "de fault" of your lawyer, you may have a malpractice case.

Defendant—A person, being sued or prosecuted for a crime, who feels like he or she has been hit by a ton of bricks.

Deposition—Oral testimony given in a lawyer's office in front of a court reporter. A "civilized" form of hand-to-hand combat.

*pleasant—like being slapped around while your hands are tied behind your back.

Discipline—What the Bar Association does to misbehaving lawyers . . . just about the time they are ready to retire.

Discovery—A legal form of "invasion of privacy." The time-consuming process by which the lawyers learn everything about the other side's case.

Due Process of Law—Guarantees written into the Constitution, which you must be given . . . before you can be legally screwed.

Ethics—Standards of conduct demanded of lawyers, which keep the game honest and true. Six fouls and they're out. (see DISCIPLINE)

Evidence—Information which lawyers seek either to present or suppress . . . depending on whether it's true.

Expert Witness—Professionals (doctors, auto mechanics, psychologists, etc.) who are paid to give their opinions in court. Some cynics claim that their opinion depends on who's paying.

Fees—A four-letter word used by lawyers to describe the money you pay them for services rendered. You probably have some four-letter words of your own.

Fiduciary—A person who owes another the highest duty of loyalty and care . . . usually because he or she is paid for it.

Hearsay—A statement made *out of court* which someone *in court* tries to introduce as evidence— inevitably followed by the other attorney immediately jumping to his or her feet and yelling "Objection, hearsay!"

Hereafter, Heretofore, Hereinabove, Hereinbelow, Etc.—Classic legalese used by lawyers to show how precise they can be, as in

"Hereinabove, please find the definition of 'hereinabove'."

Injunction—Court order prohibiting conduct, the violation of which constitutes "contempt of court." (see CONTEMPT OF COURT)

Instrument—No, not a trombone . . . a written document.

Inter Alia—A fancy Latin phrase used by lawyers to impress each other. Translation: "among other things."

Interrogatory—A modern form of torture. Interrogatories are written questions to be answered under oath in writing. Rarely found in bunches of less than 200.

Jurisdiction—Jurisprudence's younger brother. This refers to the power of the court to act, as in "exercising jurisdiction."

Jurisprudence—A fancy way of saying "the entire field of law."

Laches (pronounced "latches")—A doctrine which prevents action from being taken because of the passage of time. Almost made famous by a line from THE TREASURE OF THE SIERRA MADRE, "Laches? We don't need no stinkin' laches." But then they changed the movie from a courtroom drama to a Western, and the rest is history.

Law Clerk—An eager beaver law student who performs the "garbage work" the lawyer doesn't want to do.

Legal Secretary—Overworked and underpaid, lawyers would be helpless without them. They are the power behind the throne.

Lien (pronounced "lean")—A document you sign which gives someone else a piece out of the proceeds of your case. Hence the expression "we all need someone to lien on."

Liquidated Damages—Damages which one party agrees in advance to pay another in the event they breach a contract. Also, another name for Dean Martin's bar tab.

Litigant—A party to a lawsuit. Closely associated with "indigent," which many litigants become.

Mandatory Settlement Conference—A meeting between a judge and lawyers to try and settle your case, during which you may be told (after four years of effort), that you have a "snowball's chance in hell" of winning.

Misdemeanor—A less serious crime than a felony, yet more serious than violating an ordinance. Designed to suit the needs of the moderately crooked.

Motions—Requests made to a judge in court which take about two hours and fifteen minutes—the two hours being for time spent sitting and waiting in court.

Nolo Contendre—The fancy Latin phrase for pleading "no contest" in a criminal case. A less painful way to say "guilty as hell."

Order to Show Cause—(O.S.C.) When you have to appear in court to "show cause" why certain orders shouldn't be made. Frequently utilized in divorce cases before trial as warm-ups for the Big Event.

Offer—The terms proposed by someone wishing to make a contract. Usually met with a counter offer, which seeks to change the original proposal—unless the offer is one which cannot be refused, in which case . . . see Don Corleone for further details.

Own Recognizance—Being freed from jail without having to post bail because you had been such a fine upstanding citizen—before your true colors were shown.

Perjury—The felony of lying while under oath. Something "unethical" people frequently practice yet rarely get caught doing—unless they've worked for President Nixon.

Plaintiff—The person who brings a lawsuit. Plaintiffs rarely know what they are getting into.

Pleading—A generic term for all of the formal documents filed with a court during a lawsuit. Pleadings come in many varieties, usually long.

Precedent—A rule of law used by an Appellate Court. Must be used by other courts—unless they can figure a way around it.

Preemptory Challenge—A device where a lawyer can have a juror dismissed from the case for any reason (or no reason at all). Used by lawyers to try to shape the jury in their image.

Preliminary Hearing—A pre-trial hearing in serious criminal cases which determines whether there is enough evidence to hold a trial. In notorious cases, used by the press to convict defendants in the headlines.

Press Release—What some lawyers issue the minute they are retained by a famous client.

Presumption—A policy of law which presumes certain things are true even if they really are not.

Probation—What we give to convicted felons because our jails are overcrowded.

Procedure—The rules which govern how things are to be done, which can frequently lead to "losing the forest for the trees."

REASONABLE MAN

Reasonable Man, The—A fictional person made up by lawyers to judge human conduct, as in "Under the same circumstances, a reasonable man would have . . ." Of course, "reasonable men" always have the benefit of hindsight, so they usually would have acted just the opposite of the way you did.

Relevance—Facts must be "relevant," i.e.,"pertaining to the case," in order to be admitted into evidence.

Res (pronounced "race") Judicata—A matter, settled by a judgment, which cannot be brought up again. Also a 10K race open only to judges.

Restraining Order—A court order preventing one person from taking certain action in connection with another. Sort of the human equivalent to a dog owner's command to "heel!"

Requests for Admissions—A form of discovery which forces one to "admit" or "deny" that facts set forth in the request are true. Also used by jealous spouses who don't trust their mates.

Settlement—The resolution of a lawsuit which usually makes neither side happy.

Statute—A written law enacted by a legislative body; a derivative of statue, or "set in concrete."

Subpoena—A word even lawyers can't spell without using a dictionary. A document which tells you to appear in court.

Summons—A court document which tells you that you've been sued—and the time which you have to do something about it. Summons are always found in the company of Complaints. (see COMPLAINT)

Tort—Civil wrongs (other than breach of contract) for which redress is sought in court.

Unilateral—A one-sided act.

Verification—Lawyer slang for signing a document under penalty of perjury.

A FINAL COMMENT

Well, that about wraps it up. So, I suppose, this is where I am expected to write a clever summary that contains in one paragraph all of the "pearls of wisdom" I have been trying to give you in 200+ pages of text. This isn't easy; after all, I am a lawyer, so "short winded" is not my strong suit—but here goes. . . .

The key to a successful relationship with a lawyer is *communication*, and communication is definitely a two-way street. So, when you speak to your lawyer, speak from your heart *and* from your mind. Always let your lawyer know *how* you feel, and *why* you feel that way. When you *listen*, listen with an open mind—letting your ego go, while you ponder what your lawyer tells you. After all, it isn't important to be right, but to be honest—honest with others, certainly, but most especially honest with yourself.

So, good luck. May your costs be low, your lawyer honest and your cause just.

SUPPLEMENT
WHERE TO TURN FOR LAWYER DISCIPLINE IN ALL 50 STATES

No book like this is complete without a supplement, so the following is a list of the addresses and phone numbers of whom to contact in each of the fifty states, should you have an ethical complaint against your lawyer. I have also included whether each State Bar Association has a program of fee arbitrations and/or certified legal specialists.

Some local Bar Associations offer fee arbitration programs locally, in states which do not have statewide programs. So be sure to contact your County Bar Association before you assume that fee arbitration is not available to you.

The concept of licensing "certified specialists" is gaining steam throughout the nation, so the information contained here may change. Contact your County or State Bar Association for the latest information.

State	Name, Address & Phone	State Bar Sponsored Fee Arbitrations	Certified Specialists
Alabama	Alabama State Bar Center for Professional Responsibility 1019 South Perry Street Montgomery, Alabama 36104 (205) 269-1514	No	No
Alaska	Alaska Bar Association P.O. Box 279 Anchorage, Alaska 99510 (907) 272-7469	Yes	No
Arizona	State Bar of Arizona 363 North First Avenue Phoenix, Arizona 85003-1580 (602) 252-4804	Yes	Yes
Arkansas	Arkansas Bar Association 1501 N. University – Suite 364 Little Rock, Arkansas 72207 (501) 664-8658	Yes	No
California	State Bar of California 555 Franklin Street San Francisco, California 94102 (415) 561-8200	Yes	Yes
Colorado	Colorado Supreme Court Grievance Committee 600 17th Street – Suite 500 S. Denver, Colorado 80202 (303) 893-3393	Yes	No

State	Name, Address & Phone	State Bar Sponsored Fee Arbitrations	Certified Specialists
Connecticut	Connecticut Bar Association I was told by a representative of the State Bar of Connecticut that there is no centralized disciplinary board in that state, and that Connecticut clients who have an ethical complaint with their attorneys should contact the Superior Court in their county. For further information, contact the Connecticut Bar Association (203) 721-0025	Yes	No
Delaware	Board on Professional Responsibility Supreme Court of Delaware 12th & Market Street P.O. Box 1347 Wilmington, Delaware 19899 (302) 736-3059	Yes	No
Florida	The Florida Bar Grievance Department Tallahassee, Florida 32301-8226 (904) 222-5286	No	Yes
Georgia	State Bar of Georgia Georgia Justice Center 84 Peachtree Street, N.W. – 11th Floor Atlanta, Georgia 30303 (404) 522-6262	Yes	No
Hawaii	Hawaii Office of Disciplinary Counsel Supreme Court of the State of Hawaii 1164 Bishop Street – Suite 600 Honolulu, Hawaii 96813 (808) 521-4591	Yes	No
Idaho	Idaho State Bar P.O. Box 895 204 West State Street Boise, Idaho 83701 (208) 342-8958	Yes	No

State	Name, Address & Phone	State Bar Sponsored Fee Arbitrations	Certified Specialists
Iowa	Iowa State Bar Association 1101 Fleming Building Des Moines, Iowa 50309 (515) 243-3179	Yes	No
Illinois	Illinois Attorney Registration and Disciplinary Commission of the Supreme Court 203 North Wabash Avenue — Suite 1900 Chicago, Illinois 60601 (312) 346-0690	Yes	No
Indiana	Indiana Supreme Court Disciplinary Commission 814 ISTA Building 150 West Market Street Indianapolis, Indiana 46204 (317) 232-1807	Yes	No
Kansas	The Supreme Court of Kansas Room 278 – Kansas Judicial Center 301 N. 10th Street Topeka, Kansas 66612 (913) 296-2486	No	No
Kentucky	Kentucky Bar Association The Kentucky Bar Center W. Main at Kentucky River Frankfort, Kentucky 40601 (502) 564-3795	Yes	No
Louisiana	Louisiana State Bar Association Suite 600 210 O'Keefe Avenue New Orleans, Louisiana 70112 (504) 566-1600	No	No
Maine	Maine Board of Overseers of the Bar P.O. Box 1820 Augusta, Maine 04330 (207) 623-1121	Yes	No

State	Name, Address & Phone	State Bar Sponsored Fee Arbitrations	Certified Specialists
Maryland	Attorney Grievance Commission of Maryland District Court Building – Room 404 580 Taylor Avenue Annapolis, Maryland 21401 (301) 269-2791	Yes	No
Massachusetts	Massachusetts Board of Bar Overseers 11 Beacon Street Boston, Massachusetts 02108 (617) 720-0700	Yes	No
Michigan	Michigan Attorney Grievance Commission Marquette Building – Suite 256 243 West Congress Detroit, Michigan 48226 (313) 961-6585	Yes	No
Minnesota	Minnesota Lawyers Professional Responsibility Board 444 Lafayette Road – Fourth Floor St. Paul, Minnesota 55101 (612) 296-3952	Yes	No
Mississippi	Mississippi State Bar 620 North State Street – Suite 101 P.O. Box 2168 Jackson, Mississippi 39225 (601) 948-4471	Yes	No
Missouri	Missouri Bar Administration P.O. Box 349 Sedalia, Missouri 65301 (816) 826-7890	No	No

State	Name, Address & Phone	State Bar Sponsored Fee Arbitrations	Certified Specialists
Montana	Secretary, Commission on Practice Supreme Court of Montana P.O. Box 523 Livingston, Montana 59047 (406) 222-2023	Yes	No
Nebraska	Nebraska State Bar Association Roman Hruska Law Center 635 S. 14th Street Lincoln, Nebraska 68508 (402) 475-7091	Yes	No
Nevada	State Bar of Nevada 300 S. 4th Street – Suite 800 Las Vegas, Nevada 89101 (702) 382-0502	Yes	No
New Hampshire	New Hampshire Supreme Court Professional Conduct Commission 18 N. Main Street – Suite 205 Concord, New Hampshire 03301 (603) 224-5828	Yes	No
New Jersey	Supreme Court of New Jersey Office of Attorney Ethics Richard J. Hughes Justice Complex 25 W. Market Street North Wing 3rd Floor – CN 037 Trenton, New Jersey 08625 (609) 292-0875	Yes	Yes
New Mexico	Disciplinary Board of the Supreme Court of New Mexico Sandia Savings Building – Suite 712 400 Gold Southwest Albuquerque, New Mexico 87102 (505) 842-5781	Yes	No

State	Name, Address & Phone	State Bar Sponsored Fee Arbitrations	Certified Specialists
New York	New York State Bar Association One Elk Street Albany, New York 12207 (518) 463-3200 New York has several Disciplinary Committees to serve you, located throughout the State. Ask your local Bar Association for the address & phone number of the Committee you should contact.	No	No
North Carolina	North Carolina State Bar P.O. Box 25908 208 Fayetteville Street Mall Raleigh, North Carolina 27611 (919) 828-4620	Yes	Yes
North Dakota	Disciplinary Board of the Supreme Court of North Dakota P.O. Box 2297 Bismarck, North Dakota 58502 (701) 224-3348	Yes	No
Ohio	Office of Disciplinary Counsel of the Supreme Court of Ohio 175 South Third Street – Room 280 Columbus, Ohio 43215 (614) 461-0256	No	No
Oklahoma	Oklahoma Bar Association P.O. Box 53036 State Capitol Station 1901 North Lincoln Boulevard Oklahoma City, Oklahoma 73152 (405) 524-2365	No	No
Oregon	Oregon State Bar 1776 Southwest Madison Street Portland, Oregon 97205 (503) 224-4280	Yes	No

State	Name, Address & Phone	State Bar Sponsored Fee Arbitrations	Certified Specialists
Pennsylvania	The Disciplinary Board of the Supreme Court of Pennsylvania District I Office North American Building – Suite 310 121 South Broad Street Philadelphia, Pennsylvania 19107 (215) 735-2700	No	No
	District II Office One Montgomery Plaza – Suite 502 Swede and Airy Streets Norristown, Pennsylvania 19401 (215) 277-2224		
	District III Office Commerce Building – Suite 300 300 North 2nd Street Harrisburg, Pennsylvania 17101 (717) 232-7525		
	District IV Office 1010 Manor Complex 564 Forbes Avenue Pittsburgh, Pennsylvania 15219 (412) 391-3922		
Rhode Island	Disciplinary Board of the Supreme Court of Rhode Island 250 Benefit Street – 9th Floor Providence, Rhode Island 02903 (401) 277-3270	Yes	No
South Carolina	Commission on Grievances and Discipline 1231 Gervais P.O. Box 11330 Columbia, South Carolina 29211 (803) 758-7172	Yes	Yes

State	Name, Address & Phone	State Bar Sponsored Fee Arbitrations	Certified Specialists
South Dakota	State Bar of South Dakota 222 E. Capitol Pierre, South Dakota 57501 (605) 224-7554	No	No
Tennessee	The Board of Professional Responsibility of the Supreme Court of Tennessee 1101 Kermit Drive – Suite 405 Nashville, Tennessee 37217 (615) 361-7500	Yes	No
Texas	State Bar of Texas P.O. Box 12487 – Capitol Station Austin, Texas 78711 (512) 463-1391	No	Yes
Utah	Utah State Bar Office of the Bar Counsel 425 East 1st South Salt Lake City, Utah 84111 (801) 531-9077	Yes	No
Vermont	Vermont Professional Conduct Board c/o Office of State Court Administration State Office Building – Post Office Montpelier, Vermont 05602 (802) 828-3281	Yes	No
Virginia	Virginia State Bar Grievance Department Suite 1000 – 801 E. Main Street Richmond, Virginia 23219 (804) 786-2061	No	No

State	Name, Address & Phone	State Bar Sponsored Fee Arbitrations	Certified Specialists
Washington	Washington State Bar Association 505 Madison Street Seattle, Washington 98104 (206) 622-6026	Yes	No
West Virginia	The West Virginia State Bar E400 State Capitol Charleston, West Virginia 25305 (304) 348-2456 – Ext. 5	No	No
Wisconsin	State Bar of Wisconsin Board of Attorney's Professional Responsibility 110 E. Main Street – Room 406 Madison, Wisconsin 53703 (608) 267-7274	Yes	No
Wyoming	Wyoming State Bar Grievance Commission P.O. Box 109 Cheyenne, Wyoming 82003-0109 (307) 632-9278	Yes	No

For residents of
The District of
Columbia, contact: The Office of Bar Counsel
Building A – Room 127
515 5th St., N.W.
Washington, D.C. 20001
(202) 638-1501

If you have questions, you can also contact:
American Bar Association
Center for Professional Responsibility
750 N. Lake Shore Drive
Chicago, Illinois 60611
(312) 988-5000